G000128852

Wow Moments
A Compilation of Tantalising Tales and
Compelling Anecdotes from a Far-Flung Traveller

Lynda Gordon

Grosvenor House
Publishing Limited

This book is published by
Grosvenor House Publishing Ltd
Link House
140 The Broadway, Tolworth, Surrey, KT6 7HT.
www.grosvenorhousepublishing.co.uk

A CIP record for this book
is available from the British Library

ISBN 978-1-83975-008-3

Contents

Foreword

By Mike Lavery

In this book, Lynda takes the reader on a journey of delight to many corners of our planet and its wonders. This is no yawn-inducing travel book. Oh no, it is a collection of sharp and amusing insights into places which are inhabited by the world´s most interesting creatures and fascinating people.

The article "Geysers, Mud and the Bear Man", for example, just begs to be opened and read with relish. No condiments are needed to spice up Lynda´s amazing observations and colourful comments throughout the book. Fifty tasty tales to whet your appetite for a journey to Paradise Lost.

Lynda glides from the Highlands to the Himalayas, with the grace of an albatross and the elegance of a dolphin, with an eagle eye for the quirky and curious. She will personally introduce the reader to creatures great and small, all in their natural environment. No zoos is good news for these amazing creations.

Read "Wow Moments" in the comfort of your armchair or pack your bags and head for the hills, deserts, jungles and plains of our wonderful world.

Mike Lavery, ex-soldier with the Royal Engineers, ship´s writer and world voyager with the Merchant Navy, linguist, international leadership and management trainer and author of educational books mostly concerning the creative use of media in the classroom. He is a contributor to professional journals and local press. Mike is a fun lover and writes silly stories. He lives in Düsseldorf, Germany.

Preface

I have always had a passion for travelling to remote, far-flung places, the more off-the-beaten-track the better. During my adventures over the years, I have had the privilege to see and experience many wonderful and exciting things. Having written detailed travelogues for my own personal use, I had the notion, spurred on by many friends, to extract some of the special "wow" moments from these to compile into a book.

Having trawled my way through volumes of travelogues, scrutinised many photograph albums and given much thought to the project, I picked fifty of the most exciting, unusual, funny and/or especially beautiful or moving occurrences that I had experienced. Once started, more ideas flowed and the project came to life, resulting in this compilation of tantalising tales and compelling anecdotes.

I am also an enthusiastic photographer, always seeking to improve and develop my skills. Forty of my photos have found their way into this book to illustrate the narratives.

Hopefully this collection of compelling tales will not only entertain but also inspire readers to explore the far-flung, remote parts of our beautiful planet and seek their own "wow moments".

Introduction

A "wow moment" occurs when something exciting, unusual, funny and/or especially beautiful or moving happens unexpectedly. My travels to remote parts of the world over many years have provided a multitude of "wow moments". Many of the short stories in this compilation describe exciting encounters with wildlife whilst others tell of magical moments that transpired in a surprising variety of situations.

All 50 stories in this collection are substantially true. Most are illustrated with a photograph. Some tell of a hilariously funny moment, others describe a thing of great beauty, some relate an exciting incident whilst still others recount an event that I found deeply moving.

It is not my intention in this compilation to bombard the reader with facts or statistics, although some stories do contain factual information about the location and/or the wildlife I encountered. Instead, the key aim is to entertain and hopefully inspire the reader to explore the far-flung, remote parts of our beautiful planet and seek their own "wow moments".

Read about the elephant that invaded my tent's shower compartment in the middle of the night, the bull that tried to join me for afternoon tea, the albatross that reprimanded me for inadvertently sitting on its nest, the racoon that turned my bathroom upside-down, and many more curious or exhilarating encounters with wild creatures.

Other "wow moments" include a dazzling display of giant shimmering icebergs, New Year celebrations watching sunrise over the Himalayas, the village high in the Andes that brought tears to my eyes and pieces of fiery rock exploding into the night sky.

Happy reading!

1. Cute, Cuddly and Curious: Botswana, at the edge of the Kalahari Desert

Early mornings on the unpronounceable Makgadikgadi Pan at the edge of the Kalahari Desert can be surprisingly cold during the dry season. Hastily downing an early coffee, I boarded our four-wheel drive vehicle to venture out into the desert. In this part of Botswana, several families of meerkats have been habituated – i.e. through the patient efforts of local people, they have gradually become accustomed to the presence of human beings such that visitors can spend time in their company - up close and personal - without disturbing them. I was looking forward immensely to this experience and the very early start in the cold and dark was no deterrent.

We drove silently for a short distance. Ahead of us, light had begun to flow into the horizon, heralding the dawn. "We're here" announced our driver, stating the obvious - as the vehicle had already stopped. I peered out into the lunar landscape, wondering exactly where we were.

Daylight arrived quickly as the sun burst over the horizon. We walked silently over the rough sandy ground for a few minutes before arriving at a place where nothing at all appeared to be going on. "This is the meerkats' burrow" said our guide, confidently pointing at a big hole in the ground just ahead. "We just need to wait for them to wake up".

Meerkats, like people, don't much like cold mornings. Who can blame them? It was, however, becoming imperceptibly warmer as the sun began to climb the ink-blue sky. Suddenly, a movement. First one, then another, and moments later several meerkats emerged from the burrow. Each stood upright on its hind legs, shivering in the cool dawn and ignoring us completely. They stand upright like this to expose a bare patch of skin on their underbellies which acts to absorb the sun's rising heat.

"They're so tiny", exclaimed one of my fellow travellers. Meerkats are only about 18 inches tall (plus a long tail) and weigh just a few pounds. "There are babies in the burrow" said our guide, "but they haven't been out yet as they're only two and a half weeks old and still too small".

As the morning advanced, more meerkats appeared and began to scamper off to forage and rummage for scorpions, insects, millipedes and other delightful delicacies. My fellow travellers followed, quietly trailing the tiny creatures. One female meerkat, on babysitting duty, remained behind to stand sentry and protect the burrow's precious contents.

Sitting on the ground, I remained alone by the burrow, although I didn't consciously know why I was doing so. Shifting position slightly, I leaned forward and squinted into the burrow. To my amazement, three tiny faces peeped out at me. I sat back, incredulous, hastily setting my camera at the ready. Almost immediately one, then two, then three tiny baby meerkats emerged impertinently from the burrow. They looked around timidly, seeing the outside world for the first time. Each was hardly as big as my hand. They crouched there, cute, cuddly and curious. My camera clicked furiously.

The babysitter, however, was not impressed.

Frowning down at the precocious babies, she decided they were far too young to be allowed out.

Picking up one of the pups by the scruff of the neck, she scuttled down into the burrow, re-appearing moments later to rescue the other two, one at a time. They were gone.

I sat back, feeling exhilarated and ridiculously emotional. What an absolute privilege to have the chance to observe and experience such a thing at close quarters. An unforgettable wow moment!

2. Hairy Highlander comes to Tea: Scottish Highlands

I have always loved photographing Highland cattle. They are so superbly photogenic with their handsome, hairy faces and huge horns.

Whilst travelling in the north-west Highlands of Scotland one late September afternoon, my husband and I stopped at a roadside café for a snack. The early autumn weather was warm and sunny (unusual for this part of the world!), so we chose a table outside which backed on to the main stone wall of the café, just at its outer corner.

On the other side of the rough car park opposite the café a number of beautiful Highland cattle were grazing. I had noticed others, browsing quietly just around the corner behind where we were now sitting enjoying a cup of tea. The cattle ranged between the traditional red colour to dark brown and even creamy-white. One particularly cute calf was almost entirely white. My camera was at the ready.....

Without warning, an enormous Highland bull materialised around the corner of the café next to where I was munching my ham sandwich.

To my astonishment, this huge hulk strode right up to our table. His shaggy face was completely covered in long hair and so it was not evident whether he was looking at me, at my sandwich or at something else entirely.

But I was quite sure it was me and so I reached out to pat his hairy head. In retrospect this might not seem to have been a very sound idea, but at the time I considered it was the right and proper thing to do.

The bull flicked his head and backed off just far enough for me to leap out of my seat and take up a position nearby from which I could take some intimate photographs, leaving my husband to fend off the huge, hairy beast.

My husband continued to sip his drink, unfazed, as the massive bull resumed his investigation of our afternoon tea. He (i.e. the bull) stuck his snuffling snout right on to the table-top and proceeded to sniff the teapot. Having established that this object wasn't edible, he strutted off nonchalantly to try his luck at another table. The occupants of this table hastily abandoned their coffee and cake and fled into the interior of the café, obviously not amused by the giant hairy intruder. But why? Highland cattle are sweet-natured, gentle and docile.....

We found this unlikely encounter to be hilarious. Who wouldn't be enchanted by a visitation from such a magnificently handsome creature?

3. A Baby Seal and Me: Galapagos Islands

Each day we would visit a different island. The coastline of Santiago (also known as San Salvador or James Island) offers the visitor black lava rocks, sea caverns and tidal pools with abundant wild life. This was Galapagos at its best.

I had the privilege to spend a morning on this wild, beautiful island. Marine iguanas stood stock-still, blending in perfectly with the black lava rocks. Several times I nearly trod on one as it was so perfectly camouflaged. Others paraded about on the rocks, looking quizzical, quaint and quite bizarre.

Farther on, deeply carved fissures in the rocks provided shelter for fur seals. The ocean spilled into these deep fissures, creating deep, clear pools for marine iguanas and seals alike to enjoy.

I spotted a lone fur seal pup frolicking in a shallow pool. The water was intensely clear and calm. I stopped to watch this tiny creature as he cavorted and darted about. The scene was irresistible. I took off my shoes, waded into the pool and sat on a conveniently placed, slightly submerged rock, oblivious and indifferent to the fact that my shorts were getting wet. Just me and the baby seal, alone in a pool. The little seal showed no fear, only curiosity.

At first he ignored me, then abruptly, he began to swim towards me – closer and closer – until he was only about a foot away.

I sat perfectly still. The seal raised his little head above the water, blew some air, twitched his whiskers and studied me with wide, soft, appealing eyes. He rolled over in the water, whirled and twirled about playfully, then returned a moment later to take a more detailed look at me.

Approaching underwater, he nosed my left foot and proceeded to swim all the way around me, nudging my waist several times as he did so. He then came back around, gazed straight at me with soulful eyes before splashing away to chase an iguana.

Sheer magic!

4. Never Get between a Hippo and its Water: Tanzania, Katavi National Park

When the African rains stop and the land begins to dry up, rivers and pools shrivel and shrink day-by-day. This makes life hard for the many thousands of wild animals that exist here. Hippos, in particular, need enough water to remain submerged during the day so as to keep cool and stay safe. It is a bizarre fact, however, that hippos can't swim!

In the remote Katavi National Park in south-west Tanzania, thousands of hippos live in the many pools and rivers. As these begin to shrink, the concentrations of hippos in each pool become progressively more dense.

Whilst on a safari adventure here, we encountered massive pods of hippos. The pools in which their barrel-shaped bodies were wallowing - in uncomfortably close proximity to each other – had transformed into muddy sludge as the rains had stopped some months earlier. They were grunting, wheezing and snorting, as well as doing unmentionable things in the thick, sludgy, smelly water.

Hippos are amongst the most dangerous animals in the world as they are grumpy, aggressive and unpredictable. Although they are very heavy and have short legs, they are capable of running surprisingly fast. Our guide had regaled us with many startling stories of hippo encounters, and in particular had impressed upon us that a person should never get between a hippo and its water. Hippos are short-sighted and, when sensing danger, will bombard straight towards the nearest water, mowing down anyone or anything in their path. It was this advice that I recalled vividly when, the next day, we were parked in our open safari vehicle near another hippo pool, gazing down at a thick throng of heaving, grunting bodies.

Suddenly, on the other side of our vehicle, a huge hippo burst out of the bush, then stopped abruptly about twenty metres away.

This was a surprise even to our guide as hippos usually remain in the water during the heat of the day.

Unfortunately, our vehicle was parked directly between the hippo and its water.

The monstrous, fat beast hesitated, snorted loudly and stomped forward as if it might charge. At the last moment, it swerved off to one side making loud, aggressive grunting noises. It thundered off into the thicket, obviously extremely displeased. Our breathing slowly returned to normal.

5. Fat, Fluffy and Furry: South Georgia

South Georgia is just about as remote as you can get. It sits alone in the stormy southern ocean, some 1,500 miles southeast of the coastline of Argentina. The main island of South Georgia is just over 100 miles long and only 25 miles across at its widest. More than half of this mountainous land is permanently ice covered. Eleven peaks rise to over 6,500 feet, their slopes furrowed with deep gorges filled with vast glaciers. The island has no permanent inhabitants although British Antarctic Survey researchers and scientists spend time there in the short polar summers along with a small number of volunteers who man the small museum and shop in Grytviken, which in times past was the main whaling settlement.

My voyage from southern Chile to South Georgia took three and a half days. I had been warned to expect high winds and much rain but instead the days were dazzling and the seas benign. The sun danced and sparkled beneath an azure sky as a tail-wind propelled the small expedition ship across the southern ocean in a sprightly fashion. Many of the 100 or so passengers remained on deck in the crystal clear sunshine thereby acquiring a healthy dose of fresh ocean air and an unhealthy degree of sunburn. We were frequently accompanied by countless sea birds including many albatrosses. These graceful birds performed aerial ballet around the ship, dancing, curving and swooping elegantly. In the clear, clean air, everything seemed somehow to be magnified.

By the early morning hours of the fourth day, we finally had in our sights the coast of South Georgia, a land firmly associated with Sir Ernest Shackleton and his famous but fateful Antarctic expedition of 1914-1916. Snow-capped jagged mountain peaks began to emerge from the hazy horizon. This place was wild, pristine and magnificent.

My excitement rose as we drew closer, accompanied now by many fur seals leaping playfully out of the water as if to form a welcoming escort. Fur seals were almost wiped out here as a result of intensive hunting, and at one point the population fell as low as only one hundred animals. More recently they have achieved an incredible population explosion and reached an estimated four million. This concentration at South Georgia is the densest aggregation of marine mammals anywhere on earth.

As we landed on the wild, rocky shore (using the ship's zodiacs - small rubber boats with outboard engines), we were confronted by incredible sights and sounds. Large, aggressive bull seals growled and lolloped forward menacingly to protect their territory and their harems. Disarmingly cute, tiny babies cast their hugely appealing wide eyes on us and bleated mournfully in between bouts of frantic playfulness. Getting across the rocky beach unscathed was a challenge!

We had arrived at the unexpectedly named Salisbury Plain, a long, rocky beach alive not only with fur seals but also with an estimated 100,000 king penguins, including hundreds of fat, fluffy, furry chicks most of which were almost as tall as their parents. "Truly awesome" was the comment of one American passenger, but this failed utterly to do justice to the scene. King penguins stand at between 28 and 39 inches tall, smaller than the closely related emperor penguins, but they are nevertheless impressive with their bright orange cheek patches and yellow-orange plumage at the tops of their chests.

One hundred thousand king penguins together in one place is mind-boggling.

Handsome adult birds paraded about, squawking and squabbling noisily. Some performed their "ecstasy dance", a comical combination of sky pointing, vigorous flipper flapping and loud whistling or squawking.

Their fat chicks – ungainly brown barrels of fluff and down – begged their parents for food. Occasionally one would approach the wrong adult and get a fierce peck for its impertinence. The chicks clearly had no fear of humans and often advanced right up to our feet, cocking their heads and staring up with quaint expressions. One raucous penguin chick waddled up to me and pecked my rubber boots, possibly harbouring the illusion that this strange over-sized person-penguin might regurgitate some fishy food for him!

This hilarious and engaging behaviour provided one of the most highly entertaining mornings I have ever experienced.

6. Salute the Train: Western China

I had been travelling in western China for a week together with seven intrepid companions, plus an English guide and a Chinese guide. We had come from Kashgar, one of the westernmost cities of China and once the terminus of four silk routes, two from the east, one from Tashkent in the west and one from Pakistan by the route I had just travelled. Now we were in the large city of Ürümqi, a major stopping point on the fabled Silk Road located in the far northwest of China and reputed to be the most distant city from any sea in the world. Being highly industrial, it is also one of the most polluted.

Happily, we left this ugly city after a short sojourn and travelled on by road to Turpan, set at the edge of the Gobi Desert. The following evening, we were due to take an overnight train out of here which would take us to Liuyuan, crossing the vast Gobi desert on the way.

I had read some very unflattering reports about Chinese trains (which I expect might be of a much higher standard nowadays than back then in 1996). I was encouraged, however, by our guide's reassurance that "our" train, the express from Ürümqi to Beijing, was brand new and very comfortable. And so, we stood on the windy station platform in anticipation of the brand new train's arrival. It was then that I noticed a number of young Chinese women, all dressed alike in neatly fitting white jackets. Curious.

We didn't have to wait long. Without warning, a huge steam engine materialised out of the gloom. It chugged slowly and noisily towards us – a very impressive sight rumbling into the windy desert station. It was the longest train I have ever seen. Immediately, the young Chinese women stepped forward in unison as if they had been wound up like clockwork. They spaced themselves out at exactly equal intervals along the platform, and stood to attention. As the train approached, they all saluted in harmony. The huge engine spluttered and hissed to a halt whilst the women continued to show their respect for the steaming monster.

Saluting a train was something I had never personally contemplated doing given the unexciting appearance of modern British trains. But this massively powerful steam engine seemed to me to be worthy of veneration. So I saluted it too.

7. Wild Dogs and Warthogs: Botswana, Okavango Delta

African wild dogs are one of my favourite animals. They can run for extended periods of time on their long, slender legs, reaching speeds of up to 40 miles per hour. We had been fortunate enough to encounter a pack of around twenty of these sociable and highly intelligent creatures who at that time were residing near one of the luxury tented camps in the Okavango Delta where I was spending a few days.

Our leader/guide, Lex, had briefed us that the dogs' usual habit involved sleeping in a shady spot during the heat of the early afternoon, then gradually waking up before setting out on an evening quest for prey. So we drove in our open safari vehicle to the dogs' chosen siesta spot – under a massive tree - and found them there snoozing and snoring contentedly. "We won't have to wait long", said Lex, "they'll soon begin to wake up".

And so it was. One by one, the dogs stirred from their slumbers and began to greet each other with affectionate licking and endearing squealy noises. Once this ceremony had been completed, they began to look around.

On the top of a small hill on the other side of our vehicle, a family of around ten warthogs, including four babies, was resting, blissfully unaware of the dogs. "Wild dogs won't hunt warthogs", Lex announced, "they know that their tusks can cause serious injury".

One of the wild dogs, a large female, obviously hadn't paid any attention to what Lex had said.

She advanced slowly and positioned herself behind the front left-hand wheel of our vehicle, cleverly using it as cover.

She crouched there and fixed her gaze on the warthogs, ears pricked.

Suddenly she rose slightly, and adopted a stalking posture, focussed and resolute.

"She's going to go for it" I said in excited anticipation.

Moments later, all mayhem and havoc broke loose. Our dog hurtled out from behind the vehicle and charged up the hill at full speed, followed by the entire pack, all eagerly yapping, yipping and yelping. Shocked warthogs bolted in every direction, snorting and grunting in complete disarray. It was bedlam. Our driver propelled the vehicle up the hill in pursuit of the fleeing animals as fast as he could – we had to hang on tightly as we were bumped and jolted in every direction.

It quickly became obvious that the dogs had succeeded in their quest. High-pitched, ear-piercing squealing noises revealed that two baby warthogs had met a very sudden end.

Wild dogs, like other predators, need to eat to live. It's harsh, but it's nature.

8. The Whale that Smiled: Antarctica

We left Ushuaia during the long light of a southern summer evening and headed east along the Beagle Channel towards open ocean and a very special adventure.

Daylight by now was lasting virtually all day and night – even though the sun set for about four hours each night, it never really got dark. The two-day voyage across the infamous Drake Passage was delightfully calm with boundless sunshine. Eventually, land was sighted. We had finally arrived at Antarctica with a week in hand to explore this remote, pristine wilderness.

That evening, we were briefed by Dennis, our expedition leader (affectionately known as Dennis the Menace) and the ship's captain, Captain Paschkov (renamed Captain Passion by some of the female passengers ... don't ask why! ...). Dennis the Menace divulged that, due to exceptionally favourable weather and sea conditions, it had been decided to alter the ship's planned itinerary and instead head south as far as conditions would allow, with the aim of crossing the Antarctic Circle and reaching an area called Marguerite Bay, normally beyond the reach of a ship without ice-breaking capacity.* How exciting!

The following night, our ship gently crunched its way through ice floes, heading ever southwards. The next morning, the clarity of light and mirror-calm of the ocean were stunning. On our port side, high mountain peaks carved out of black rock and partly coated with white snow dominated the ocean whilst ahead of us massive glistening icebergs loomed up like sculpted castles. The sea was so startlingly clear that the under-sides of the bergs could be seen gleaming bright blue or aquamarine below the surface.

By mid-afternoon, we had crossed the Antarctic Circle with a triumphant whoop and celebratory vodka. Later in the afternoon we reached Marguerite Bay, an area of extraordinary beauty. This far south, the air was so clear and sharp that everything somehow seemed to be magnified.

Ahead of us we could see a group of humpback whales lolling around on the sea surface. "The whales are chilling out" said Dennis the Menace, they must have fed well and are just enjoying the lovely sunshine, as indeed we were.

After a quick change of plan, our captain altered course slightly and slowly advanced towards the whales. The expedition staff soon had the passengers loaded, eight to a boat, on to the ship's zodiacs (small inflatables with outboard engines) cruising very gently towards the whales. The sea was like rippled silk, rendered golden in the rays of the low sun.

Once we arrived closer to the whales, my boat driver switched the engine off and we floated quietly, feeling energised and excited.

Around 25 humpback whales were relaxing in the sunlight-strewn sea. We floated amongst them in our small boats as they surfaced, turned themselves upside-down, fluked their huge tails and slapped their fins on the sea surface.

Humpback whales average 50 feet in length and I was in an 18-foot open boat. But humpbacks are gentle and highly intelligent, and our expert expedition staff knew they would not harm us, even at such close quarters. As we watched, it seemed as if the whales were deliberately putting on a playful performance just for us.

But the best was still to come. I spotted a whale on the surface directly approaching our zodiac from the port side. Closer and closer he came. Then he dived down under the boat. Turning around quickly, I caught sight of his huge head, still under the surface of the water, now on the starboard side. He was directly underneath us, half a whale on one side and half on the other side of the little boat. Then he disappeared. "Where did he go?" someone asked. We waited and watched in silence, looking all around for the disappeared whale. Then it happened. The whale's giant head rose up from the water - ever so slowly - less than a metre from my sea-level position in the zodiac. Everyone in the boat gasped. The whale seemed to be looking directly at me and in my imagination I knew that he was smiling.

After a few seconds, the whale slid vertically back down into the water in slow motion, and incredibly, created hardly a ripple on the sea surface. "Awesome" said one fellow-passenger, but this description didn't, and couldn't, come anywhere close to describing the experience.

* *Footnote:* This voyage took place in 1995, many years before climate change began to cause Antarctica's sea-ice to melt back each summer beyond the Antarctic Circle. We were told later that we were the first ever non-ice-breaker passenger ship to make it this far south.

9. The Road was Long and Steep: Pakistan, Karakoram Highway

Back in 1996, at a time when it was safe to travel in northern Pakistan, I undertook a week-long road journey from Rawalpindi northwards along the 500 miles of the Karakoram Highway, then up and over the Khunjerab Pass into southern China. The route traces one of the many paths of the ancient Silk Road.

At first the scenery was lush and green with rolling hills enfolding steep valleys. Pine trees and diverse crops grew side by side – rice, fruit, maize and tea seemed to co-exist happily.

Hotchpotch villages gave me and my seven fellow travellers an insightful glimpse of rural Pakistan. Many villages were inhabited by refugees from Afghanistan – tall, elegant, bearded men wearing white turbans – all with a smile and welcoming demeanour. Few women folk were to be seen and those one or two whom we did see were heavily veiled, staring apprehensively out from behind dark folds of cloth.

Brightly painted buses overflowed with people, even more brightly painted trucks laboured noisily up steep hills whilst the occasional remnants of a landslide slowed us a little on our northerly route.

Further up the highway, in order to link neighbouring hill villages on opposite sides of the Indus river, the people had in some places built primitive cable-car contraptions. A few of us had an unexpected experience of one, as we were invited to be hauled high up over the raging river canyon in a completely open-at-the sides tubular wooden apparatus! Scary!

The next day, after a storm, the air was fresh, the hills were green and our Pakistani guide proclaimed that the mountains were "happy". As the highway continued to climb, the scenery became ever more rugged. The river Indus steamed and boiled its tortuous course at the foot of avalanche-strewn mountain-sides. Now we were entering the land of remote hill-tribal peoples who did not regard themselves as Pakistani, did not pay taxes and were reputed to (occasionally) hold up and rob (although not harm) people in passing vehicles.

The Karakoram Highway was built by the military between 1956 and 1979. Over 1,000 workers died during its construction mainly as a result of blasting operations and avalanches.

The road is regularly blocked by landslides of which we saw evidence of many, and hints of many more yet to come.*

There was little traffic now, apart from the occasional colourful truck.

Apart from the "happy" mountains, we encountered happy cows along these lower valleys – "happy" because their main diet was wild cannabis which grew profusely along both sides of the road!

Each day we travelled higher and higher – now the greenery diminished as the mountains became steeper and rockier.

The road in places was extremely narrow with sharp twists and turns and steep sides, affording vertical views of the raging river below. Wild mint, fluffy pink tamarisk and bright lavender grew in the valley, giving off beautifully pungent perfumes. In the afternoon, we stopped to pluck ripe apricots directly from some fruiting trees.

Next day we passed through the stunningly beautiful green and fertile Hunza Valley with a different view of snow-capped mountain peaks at every corner, one thrusting up behind the other. Continuing our journey, we began to climb more steeply, still making our way alongside the tumbling river. Here and there, our driver had to steer around boulders which had crashed on to the road from the sheer slopes above us. We were heading for the Khunjerab Pass, which at approximately 15,466 feet, is one of the highest road passes in the world.

Finally at the top, we left Pakistan and the Karakoram Highway behind and after a five-hour drive through a virtual "no-man's land" and various curious and tedious immigration formalities, passed into China. Soon the high Himalayan peaks began to recede into the distance behind us as the land opened out into a wide, flat plain which alternated between grassland and semi-desert.

The road from Pakistan into China was long and steep, but my week-long journey up and over the Karakoram Highway was one of the most adventurous, stimulating and fascinating experiences of my life.

* Footnote: Following a massive landslide upstream from the Hunza valley in 2010, part of the northern Karakoram Highway has been completely rebuilt.

10. Stalked: Botswana, Okavango Delta

I have lyricised elsewhere about the admirable qualities of African wild dogs and how intelligent and sociable they are. On this occasion, I was enjoying an evening safari drive during which we were attempting to trail a pack of wild dogs through thick bush. The dogs were trotting along industriously, hunting for suitable prey. We were tagging along at a steady pace. For no particular reason, I happened to glance behind. A lone spotted hyena was trailing the rear of our safari vehicle. On and on he came, following persistently in our path. We were being stalked!

After a while, our driver stopped the vehicle as we had temporarily lost sight of the wild dogs.

Our four-legged follower, however, kept coming and tramped right up to the left side of our open-sided vehicle, brushing against the front wheel.

He looked intently up at me.

For a moment I deliberated reaching down to pat his head, but quickly recognised that this would be highly inadvisable - hyenas' jaws are so strong that they can bite through bone and I didn't much fancy having my hand amputated!

It was then that I noticed that several more hyenas were moseying along behind us. Our guide explained that hyenas often follow wild dogs as they know that the dogs are highly efficient and successful hunters and hope that they will have the opportunity to steal their kill. Realisation dawned – the hyena wasn't stalking me after all, he was following the wild dogs. But where were they?

Suddenly, chaos broke out. A terrified young antelope fled past our vehicle pursued hotly by squealing wild dogs. Almost immediately, the unfortunate antelope met a sudden end. The dogs began to chomp noisily into their dinner as the hyenas looked on enviously, now forming a small circle around the pack of dogs.

We watched with fascination as our very own stalker cunningly and craftily sneaked up close to the wild dogs and made devious attempts to make a grab for a piece of the meat. The dogs weren't having any of it. As they outnumbered the hyenas, they were able to fend them off, although not without a great deal of raucous howling and yowling. The dogs' favourite technique seemed to be to take a nip at a hyena's backside, causing it to yelp loudly and scuttle off. Of course, wild dogs can only do this if they outnumber the hyenas as they are much smaller; a wild dog on its own would have no chance of winning the battle against a single hyena. On this occasion the wild dogs numbered around sixteen and there were only about five hyenas.

The hyenas, on this occasion, went hungry.

11. Soft and Dense: Madagascar, Andasibe-Mantadia National Park

Madagascar is a land beyond imagination. Its fascination lies in the fact that over 90% of all its animal and plant species are found nowhere else on earth. Almost all of Madagascar's reptile and amphibian species, half of its birds, and all of its lemurs are endemic to the island. The lemurs - primates which are unrelated to monkeys (they developed separately and are thought to be descended from African bush babies) - are extremely endearing.

Towards the east coast of central Madagascar lies the Andasibe-Mantadia National Park. Here, deep in the heart of the rainforest sits the Vicôna Forest Lodge, a delightful oasis near a beautiful lake with bungalows set in landscaped gardens amidst undulating forest trails. During three days here, I concluded that this was the most beautiful and atmospheric rainforest I had ever visited – the variety of trees, bushes, ferns, bamboo and other plants was mind-boggling – all with differing shapes, heights, habits and textures.

Near the Vicôna Forest Lodge, a small island, known as "Lemur Island" is open to visitors. The island sits in a lake and access is by small boat, chauffeured by local people, across a channel that is only a few metres wide. Four species of lemur inhabit Lemur Island – black and white ruffed, common brown, bamboo and Diademed Sifaka. Lemurs, apparently, don't like water and so the lemurs here are permanent residents.

Over a period of time, these lemurs have been "habituated", i.e. they have gradually become accustomed to people and so visitors can approach them closely without disturbing them in any way. So used are these lemurs to people that some of them have developed the habit of using human heads and shoulders as posts and pillars on which to perch, or from which to spring to the next tree or alternatively on to the nearest unsuspecting human being.

I was first off the boat. In my enthusiasm for these endearing, engaging creatures, I immediately crouched down to photograph a brown lemur on the path directly in front of me. Then – thump! I didn't see it coming. A lemur had jumped on to the top of my head. My companions laughed hysterically. But that was just the start of a highly entertaining afternoon. These gentle lemurs treated us with complete indifference – choosing to leap unceremoniously on to heads, shoulders or arms, sometimes two or three at a time. They were gorgeous.

When an especially beautiful black and white ruffed lemur jumped on to my right shoulder, I tentatively reached over with my left hand to touch it.

Wow! I have never felt fur so superbly soft and dense. My fingers penetrated deep into exquisite softness.

I subsequently pondered why an animal that lives in a hot country would have such thick, dense fur. I have never discovered the answer.

12. Joseph and the Bucket Shower: Southern Tanzania

Southern Tanzania is much less touristic, less busy and less developed than the ever-popular Serengeti in the north of this wild and wonderful country. My travels here took me into Katavi National Park, a remote park in the south-west of the country that is less frequently visited than other Tanzanian national parks. Accommodation here was a large, well-furnished tent. No hot and cold running water though. Nevertheless, showering was available in a private area at the back of the tent, accessible through a canvas "door" from the tent's main "bedroom".

This area was screened off on three sides with flimsy bamboo walls which barely reached five feet in height. There was no roof.

Within this area stood a basic pulley contraption from which a large metal bucket hung. Rudimentary pipework led from the bucket to a shower head poised above the open showering area.

This was our "bucket shower", an ingenious method of ensuring cleanliness without the need for either electricity or running water.

It works as follows: you are asked what time of day you would like your shower. At the appointed time, a member of the camp staff arrives, lowers the pulley and fills your bucket with fresh hot water. He then hoists the bucket up to the appropriate height, shouts "hello, shower ready" or something similar, and departs.

The system is delightfully simple. You pull a rope that hangs down from the bucket – this opens small holes at the bottom of the bucket allowing the water to spray out – just like a real shower. If you want the water to stop, you simply pull the rope again. The challenge for me was to work out whether and when there was enough water left in the bucket to shampoo my long hair, wash out the conditioner and wash myself down as well!

The camp manager had briefed us well about the merits of the bucket shower and had also warned us to make sure to always empty all the water out of the bucket. Why? "There are many elephants in this area" he said: "They won't trouble you, so don't worry. But there's one elephant in particular, a young bull we call Joseph who frequently wanders around the camp at night and has a habit of trying to drink water out of the buckets!"

That night I heard some odd noises. Not to worry, we had been assured that the elephants would not trouble us. Suddenly awake, I sat bolt upright and looked out through the mesh "window" at the side of the tent. A large, dark silhouette slowly moved past. Joseph! There followed some strange noises – a low thud, a clonk, a scuffling sound. Moments later he was gone and the African night's peace and quiet resumed.

Early the next morning, my husband rose for his shower – having requested it at the ludicrously early and dark hour of 5.30am. Moments later various muffled murmurings and mutterings floated through into the main area of the tent. "This b****** shower won't work" cried an exasperated voice. "It's giving me only a tiny dribble of water". Emerging uncleansed and frustrated, my husband was not amused when he found me laughing heartily at his misfortune, guessing what calamity had afflicted the bucket.

And I guessed right. Later, the camp staff mended the bucket contraption, regaling us with the story of Joseph's visit to the camp the previous night and his re-adjustment of our shower mechanism.

Now my husband loves to entertain our friends with the story of an elephant called Joseph who visited our tent in the middle of the African night and wreaked havoc on our shower.

13. Joseph and the Gin and Tonic: Southern Tanzania

Remote Katavi National Park in southern Tanzania sports large numbers of elephants. The park lies a little east of the lovely Lake Tanganyika and it was here that we spent a delightful few days with accommodation in a comfortable tented camp. Evenings were particularly agreeable. After the excitement of a day on safari, we would gather in a circle around the bright, welcoming campfire for a while before dinner, enjoying a bit of banter with fellow guests and camp staff. Drinks were served – Chardonnay (my favourite tipple)?, whisky? gin and tonic? Whatever you fancy.

The camp manager had warned us that elephants frequently wandered through the camp at night, and that one bull elephant in particular was a regular visitor. Guess who? Joseph again!

"Joseph is no problem", the camp manager said, "he comes around often and he's very laid-back".

Our campfire pleasantries were suddenly interrupted by untypical scuffling noises emanating from the nearby bush. Joseph! Joseph's bulky silhouette materialised out of the darkness just a few metres behind the circle of chairs which surrounded the campfire. Obviously he had decided that he wanted to join us. "He probably wants a beer", my husband pronounced. "Give him a bucket of gin and tonic", suggested a fellow guest.

Joseph flapped an ear and emitted a low rumbling noise – that wonderfully distinctive and characteristic sound that elephants make in order to communicate. "No", replied the camp manager, "he said he prefers to drink the water out of the shower buckets". [See previous article "Joseph and the Bucket Shower"]. We all laughed and continued to watch Joseph's huge profile illuminated by the glow of the campfire.

Joseph, however, seemed unimpressed by our various comments and continued chomping rowdily on a nearby bush. We watched him in silence, marvelling at how implausibly close we were to a full-sized wild African elephant. Moments later, presumably satisfied that his antics had caused sufficient entertainment, he moved off, dissolving silently into the night. He was gone! Wow!

14. Little Pet Puffin: Iceland

Everybody loves puffins. Cute and comical, their absurdly bright orange bills and feet create huge appeal and surely make them Britain's most loved seabird.

Whilst travelling in Iceland, I decided to visit a small folk museum in a little island community. It was rumoured that the lady who ran the museum had a pet puffin. I considered this to be somewhat unlikely, however on enquiring at the museum's reception, the lady said "O yes, he's wandering about somewhere upstairs". Bemused, I proceeded upstairs, spurning the opportunity to admire the fascinating artefacts, historic photographs and enlightening information boards that had been painstakingly displayed.

In a small room on the first floor, various wall displays depicted the life of ordinary folk in coastal Iceland. There was no one else in the room and it contained no furniture. Where was the puffin?

Lowering my eyes, I sensed a movement on the floor. There stood the little puffin, cheeky as you like. He looked at me disparagingly then proceeded to strut across the room as if he thought to guide me around the various displays.

The friendly lady owner appeared at the door. "You can hold him" she said.

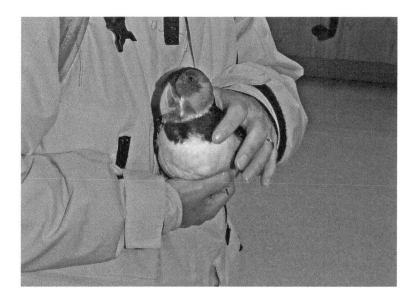

Finding this prospect irresistible, I gently picked up the tiny bird and cradled him close.

"He likes to be stroked at the back of his head" she said.

Obligingly, I caressed the tiny creature behind its "ears", in the same way as I might stroke a puppy.

Now, anyone who has ever owned a dog will have observed that when you caress it behind its ears, it will tend to cock its head to one side, close its eyes and exhibit a blissful expression. To my astonishment, this tiny, cute puffin displayed exactly the same behaviour. Its head tilted to the right, its eyes drooped sleepily and its little face looked ecstatic. It was absolutely hilarious.

The museum owner explained to me that she had rescued the puffin as an abandoned baby and raised it to adulthood. By then it was so tame and loved that she decided to keep it as a pet. The tiny creature had free run of the museum and the nearby garden, and so could, if it chose to do so, fly away to join its wild relatives on the sea cliffs. However, it had obviously decided that abandoning cosy, comfortable museum life was not such a great idea. So it had stayed, no doubt providing endless entertainment to all the museum's visitors. Especially me.

15. Mud Bath: Malawi

Earlier that day, one of the camp's staff had watered the flowering plants outside our tent. As a result, a large, muddy puddle remained, slightly hollowed into the ground.

I was enjoying a relaxing siesta, reading quietly in the shade of a huge tree when I heard a scuffling, snuffling noise. I looked up. There, just a few metres away, a large female warthog had materialised out of the bush. Behind her emerged four very small baby warthogs with delightful little piggy faces. Mrs Warthog eyed me up warily, then decided it was worth the risk. She advanced up to the muddy pool, inspected it thoroughly, then embarked on a raucous bath. She rolled on her sides, rotated on to her back and kicked her legs in the air, all the while splashing, splattering and splurging mud in all directions. Occasionally she stopped her revelling to look at me, presumably to make sure I wasn't about to launch an assault on her babies. I sat perfectly still, captivated.

At first, the four babies looked on, seemingly baffled and bewildered by Mum's strange behaviour. Then, each one in turn decided that they ought to have a go.

This was absolutely hilarious. The tiny baby warthogs tried their best to imitate their mother who continued to wallow enthusiastically in the mud.

But they couldn't quite get the hang of it.

They slipped, slid and slithered in the gooey mire, their legs thrashing uncontrollably. Many valiant attempts were made to master the art of the mud-bath, but they all finished up in flailing, fumbling failure.

The party went on for several minutes until Mum decided she had had enough. She resumed an upright position and trotted off happily back into the bush, followed speedily by her four floundering, mud-spattered infants.

16. Silent, Lonely Land: Greenland, East Coast

The east coast of Greenland is a wild, rugged place with very few settlements, due to the harshness of the climate and the stark mountainous landscape. Hence there are hundreds of miles of empty coastline indented with narrow, icy fjords, many of which are uncharted.

Here, the small expedition ship entered Skjoldungensund, a deep, narrow, horseshoe-shaped fjord that has a second entrance further down the coast. The early September weather was spectacularly fine with clear blue skies and little wind. It didn't even feel cold. This silent, lonely land was spectacular beyond imagination.

Steep-sided granite mountains with sheer, craggy rock faces soared thousands of feet upwards from the dark waters into towering, snow-capped peaks.

As we advanced up the fjord, mountain peak after mountain peak unfolded, often separated by sweeping ice-fields and massive crunching glaciers.

From these, glacier melt-water flowed in milky rivulets into the fjord.

Here and there, fields of broken glacier ice lay in our path, but our small but sturdy ship ploughed through them easily.

Crisp blue icebergs sparkled in the sunlight as they glided gracefully past our ship, and a few bearded seals poked their curious heads up out of the still water, no doubt wondering what type of strange, foreign creature was invading their waters. The land was completely empty and eerily silent. I was sure that I must be farther away from civilisation than I had ever been before as our explorations had taken us many hundreds of miles from the nearest settlement.

We went ashore somewhere for an exploratory walk. In contrast with the stark black and white of the high mountains, the autumn colours on the land near the coast were magnificent – yellow low-growing willow, red-leaved blueberry bushes, brown heather and green mosses all hugged the soft, spongy ground.

Words alone cannot properly describe the majesty of this wild and remote landscape.

Unforgettable.

17. Thief on a Tightrope: Costa Rica, Monteverde

Photographing hummingbirds in dull, wet conditions in the midst of a cloud-forest is a serious challenge. Hummingbirds are tiny and when they hover in mid-air, their wings can flap at speeds of up to 80 beats per second. This makes sharp focussing insufferably difficult. Another astonishing fact about hummingbirds is that they can fly backwards!

That day, the light was low and a constant drizzle misted down, soaking us thoroughly. Most of my travelling companions had deserted the excursion to return to our lodge, set deep in the hills of Monteverde in Costa Rica. Not to be deterred, I joined four others to walk to a location in the forest where a local gentleman regularly maintained feeders filled with nectar to attract hummingbirds. These feeders dangled at the bottom of solid wires, which in turn hung from thicker horizontal wires tied to the trunks of nearby trees.

I was discussing the merits of different camera settings in a futile attempt to achieve a sharply focussed photograph of these beautiful hummingbirds when a movement in one of the trees caught my attention. What was that? I peered through the mist up into the leafy branches. A sharp flick of a furry tail confirmed that I had not imagined it. Something was swishing about up there in the trees. What could it be?

Suddenly, the creature emerged. For a moment I thought it was a lemur but realised a mille-second later how silly this thought was since lemurs live only in Madagascar and I was on the other side of the world in Costa Rica.

The mystery creature strutted arrogantly along a low tree branch, then proceeded to do a tight-rope balancing act along the horizontal wire that led from there towards us and the hummingbird feeders. I could see now that his fur was brown, he had large eyes that filled his short, rounded face and his body was about 18 inches long with an even longer thick, bushy tail.

As I watched him, he abandoned the horizontal wire and nimbly climbed down one of the vertical wires, clutching it precariously and wrapping his long tail around it for balance.

Clinging to the wire with only his back legs and his tail, he then used both front paws to grasp the hummingbird feeder and tip it towards him.

He then proceeded to drink down the nectar.

So what was this lemur-like creature? It was a northern olingo, a member of the racoon family. Olingos are normally nocturnal, but this individual had obviously learned that it was worth staying awake during the day in order to raid the hummingbird feeders. He was now only a few feet away from where I was standing and he was absolutely beautiful.

18. Whale at Three O'clock: Scotland, somewhere in the Minch

When westerly gales blast in from the Atlantic ocean, the stretch of water (the Minch) that lies between the Highlands of Scotland and the outer Hebrides can be wild and stormy, even in summer.

My elderly mother and I caught the early morning ferry from Ullapool in the far north-west of Scotland, heading for Stornoway on the Isle of Lewis, a voyage of around two and three quarter hours. My mother had dosed herself up with seasickness pills, but as it turned out, these were entirely unnecessary. The sea was as calm as silk that morning. Not a single breath of wind rippled the surface of the water. As we approached the western isles, a light, low mist drifted on top of the sea creating the impression that the mountains ahead of us were floating.

The weather was so fine and the views so spectacular that many passengers had chosen to spend time on the outside deck. A group of somewhat scruffy young men from Glasgow were drinking pints of beer and talking noisily.

To my astonishment, I suddenly spotted a minke whale – it surfaced near the ship and almost immediately dove down again. I have always thought that minke whales are the most uninteresting of whales as they rarely remain at the surface for more than a few moments. Nevertheless I was excited to see one here in Scottish waters. I reacted immediately....

On my many far-flung expedition voyages I had been well taught how to react when sighting a whale. So that everyone else has maximum chance to see what you think you have spotted, you shout the word "whale" very loudly and identify its position by imagining the bow of the ship points to twelve o'clock and declaring what time of day the whale is at. So, for example, you would shout "whale, twelve o'clock" if the whale was directly ahead of the ship.

So ingrained was this training in my mind that on sighting the minke whale, my reaction was instinctive and automatic. "Whale, three o'clock" I cried loudly, pointing straight out to starboard.

Complete silence ensued. The now slightly inebriated youths stared at me with disbelief and disdain. Others on deck cast strange sideways glances in my direction and muttered knowingly to each other. "There was a whale – out there", I garbled, trying without success to justify my outburst, but nobody else had seen it and they all obviously thought I was a complete lunatic. The thought crossed my mind that someone would now call ahead to Stornoway and arrange for me to be met and removed by men in white coats. Even my mother was suspicious. "Yes dear", she said sweetly but unconvincingly when I insisted that I had seen a real whale.

However, this story had a happy ending. Fortunately for my reputation (and sanity), another minke whale surfaced momentarily a few minutes later. This time, the noisy Glasgow youths saw it and all immediately abandoned their pints of beer and rushed excitedly to the side of the ship, waving their arms and shouting loudly. Redeemed, I crossed my arms and smirked smugly.

19. Wild Dogs and White Wine: Botswana

I had been on safari trips before in which I felt I was very much an outsider looking in, cocooned away in comfortable lodges and enclosed touring minibuses. As exciting and wonderful as the game viewing could be, the experience of the animals was like passing an acquaintance in the street

– no in-depth relationship could be forged. There was never time, nor opportunity, to feel at one with the land, to appreciate its grandeur and wildness or to relax long enough to truly enjoy the wild animals and their endlessly fascinating behaviour. There was always a flurry of other vehicles around the animals every time we stopped to look. If ever there was a moment when an emotional link might be formed, then I was whisked away from it, and moved quickly on to the next destination.

My safari trip to Botswana was entirely different. We rarely saw another vehicle and stayed in small, remotely located tented camps which had every comfort and which were unfenced and open to the wild. Safari drives took place in spacious, open vehicles and were relaxed and unhurried. Each time we encountered animals we were able to spend as much time as we wanted in their company.

During the late afternoon safari outing each day, we would stop, get out of the vehicle and indulge in "sundowners", a delightful African custom. Whilst watching the setting sun, usually in some picturesque spot, we would enjoy chilled drinks and a canapé or two. On this particular occasion, we had stopped in an open woodland where the visibility on all sides was good, hence safe.

Earlier we had seen some wild dogs trotting off to hunt. I was standing a few feet away from the seven others in our group, sipping my glass of chilled Chardonnay and enjoying the hush of the close of day. "Look" exclaimed Lex, our guide/leader.

A hundred or so metres away, a wild dog was trotting with intent through the forest.

Furthermore, he was trotting directly towards me – closer and closer he advanced.

"Don't worry", said Lex, "he won't harm you". I quivered, mesmerised and rooted to the spot, tightly gripping my precious Chardonnay.

Lex was right of course, the beautiful wild dog had no interest in me. However, to everyone's amusement, he trotted past me at a distance of just a few feet, ignoring someone's suggestion that I might offer him a sip of my wine .....

20. Rebirth: Yungay, Peru

The bus journey took eight and a half hours. From Lima, Peru's bustling capital city, the rickety bus chugged its way north, following the coast initially then turning inland through semi-desert landscape. It began to climb, and climb, and climb, up and up through narrow gorges with high craggy mountains looming ahead, eventually passing up through the clouds. It seemed as if the bus was on the verge of touching the sky. Once over the high pass, it rumbled downhill through clear, open countryside to the small town of Huaraz, my destination for the next three days. I breathed in the beautifully clear mountain air and relaxed.

This 8,000 foot high Andean valley was beautifully green and peaceful. Next morning, pink clouds adorned the snow-white mountain peaks as I set off. Some way down the valley, I arrived at the location of Yungay, a small town which in May 1970 was completely buried in an enormous avalanche triggered by a magnitude 8 earthquake. The towering peak next to Yungay was so destabilised by the earthquake that a substantial part of its north side broke away and rumbled and roared down towards the valley at speeds of up to 200 miles per hour. As it thundered down, it gathered rubble, tore up trees and amassed boulders, glacial ice, snow and mud. Minutes later, the entire town of Yungay, together with most of its 25,000 inhabitants, was crushed and buried under metres of rocks and rubble. The Peruvian government subsequently declared the site a national cemetery and forbade excavation (instead, a new town was built further up the valley).

The only place that offered relative security for people trying to flee the avalanche was the cemetery, built above ground on an artificial hill. Around 350 Yungay inhabitants who were able to scramble up to the top of this elevated cemetery in time survived the disaster.

It was seventeen years on from the devastating avalanche when I visited Yungay.

The only visible signs of the tragedy were the engraved crosses above the spots where homes had formerly stood, the shattered remains of a church steeple and the spindly tips of four palm trees that had once graced the town's main plaza.

In stark contrast, this place of devastation and tragedy had now become a fertile green pasture full of life. Profusions of wild meadow flowers swarmed with bees and butterflies. The sun shone warmly. Birds sang through the gentle breeze. Visiting children were laughing and puppies were playing. There was an air of complete peace, calm and harmony. A rebirth.

What took me by surprise was the intensity of the emotion I felt there. On the one hand, the story of the destruction and of how people's lives had been obliterated by this cataclysmic event aroused such a deep sadness in me that tears welled from my eyes. The knowledge that entire families and their homes were buried beneath the ground on which I stood was overwhelming. On the other hand, the evidence of so much new life and the feeling of deep peace in this place evoked a feeling of joy. The contrast was extraordinary. I have never before, or since, felt such a powerful "atmosphere" in a place. It moved me very deeply.

21. Roaring in the Night, Botswana, Okavango Delta

The Okavango Delta was the 1000th site to be officially entered into the UNESCO World Heritage List. The Delta is a vast wetland created by the seasonal flooding of the Okavango River as it flows southwards from Angola into the Kalahari Desert where it unfurls over the flat ground branching out into hundreds of small streams and lakes. All the water reaching the Delta ultimately evaporates or transpires and so the river never reaches the ocean. Because the flood peaks between June and August during Botswana's dry winter months and the rainy season stretches from around December to March, the Delta is never dry. As a result, it attracts tens of thousands of wild animals and birds creating one of Africa's greatest concentrations of wildlife.

During a stay in a delightful luxury tented camp in the heart of the Okavango, I was awakened one night at around 2.00am by extra-loud hippo gruntings and frog croakings. I knew that the deep African night exaggerates animal sounds and that if you hear loud noises, the animal is usually some distance away. Or so I believed .....

I then heard the clear sound of a lion roaring, resembling a persistent, low moaning. Five minutes later, there was another roar, ostensibly much closer. I was dozing off again when I heard loud rustlings in the grass immediately in front of my tent. Without realising what I was doing, I sat bolt upright. And there, right in front of the tent, less than 20 feet away, was the clear silhouette of a very large male lion, strolling past nonchalantly. I could see him clearly as I tended not to draw the thick canvas "curtains" over the mesh front of my tent, preferring not to shut out the wonderful nature outside.

The glimpse was over in about five seconds as the lion melted into the darkness. I heard him moving away into the undergrowth with much more rustling. I wondered if I was dreaming.

In the morning, I related this tale to the rest of our small group and the camp manager. One of the camp's guides accompanied me into the grassy area in front of my tent and there was the evidence – fresh, lion paw prints right there. I had not, after all, dreamt the whole episode. Wow!

22. Reprimanded by an Albatross: Falkland Islands

Steeple Jason Island lies on the north-west fringes of the Falkland Islands and is fully exposed to the many southern Atlantic gales and storms. Landing on this island is challenging. There is no natural harbour and the coastline is rugged, rocky and ripped by fierce tides. The island rises dramatically to around 1,000 feet. It is uninhabited and protected as a nature reserve.

Steeple Jason Island is home to the largest colony of breeding black-browed albatrosses in the world – around 200,000 pairs nest here each year. These magnificent birds, which have a wingspan of up to nearly eight feet, are so called because they have a dark eye-stripe stretching out from the back of each eye.

Black-browed albatrosses build their nests on steep slopes of rock and tussock grass close to the ocean. Their nests are solid tube-shaped pillars constructed of mud and guano with some grass and seaweed thrown in for good measure. These pillars can often be a couple of feet high.

The small expedition ship on which I was travelling had permission to land its passengers on Steeple Jason Island one morning in early November (spring in the Falklands). We slogged through long tussock grass to get to the edge of one of the many breeding colonies where we sat quietly for a while observing the birds and their behaviour. Later, we had free time to walk up the hill and enjoy the view over this spectacular island.

Descending, I walked farther across the hillside a little way above the coastline to another albatross colony. I fought my way through some tall, tough tussock grass until I reached the top edge of the colony which stretched all the way from where I stood down to the edge of the ocean.

Hundreds of albatrosses were sitting contentedly on their pillars whilst others were marching up and down to and from the sea.

The birds all ignored me completely.

I spotted what looked like an abandoned pillar at the very top edge of the colony – only about a foot high, it looked deserted, derelict and disused. Perfect as a seat for me to relax and quietly commune with the birds.

After a while, I observed an individual albatross walking resolutely and relentlessly up through the colony. I watched him (or perhaps her) with interest. On and on the bird plodded, up and up, heading directly towards me. Surely he wasn't coming for me? The bird stomped and waddled on until he was only about three feet from where I was perched. He stopped and stared straight at me. From my seated position about a foot above the ground, he was taller than me. He then slowly raised his head towards the sky and brayed very loudly. My goodness, this bird was talking to me, telling me to get off his seat! I was being reprimanded!

I obeyed of course and stepped back into the tussock grass. As I watched him, he plonked himself on top of his pillar and settled down contentedly. Wow!

23. Ice Cruise: Antarctica

You have to be serious to want to travel to Antarctica. First there is a fourteen hour flight from the UK to Argentina or Chile and then another three or four hours flying south to the port of Ushuaia which sits right at the bottom of South America and is known locally as "the end of the world". After steaming out from the end of the world, there is a voyage of approximately two days across the notoriously wild Drake Passage before the wondrous ice-capped seventh continent eventually looms on the horizon. In reality Ushuaia is not the end of the world, but only the beginning.

Many people are surprised to learn that settled spells of calm, sunny weather are not unusual during the Antarctic summer. Cold – yes - but crisp and dry. In these conditions, the light is exquisite, the air is sharp and clear and somehow everything seems to be magnified.

Our small expedition ship had reached an area off the east side of the Antarctic Peninsula where many large tabular icebergs tower high above the ocean.

These flat-topped, vertical-sided slabs of freshwater ice can sometimes be several miles long.

Conditions that day were perfect - flat calm seas and dazzling sunshine. And so our expedition leader offered the passengers the opportunity to take an unplanned zodiac cruise amongst the icebergs. We set off – five zodiacs (small, inflatable open boats) coasted gently across the silken sea, heading north into the sun.

"What's that large object lying on the surface of the water?" asked one of my fellow-travellers. Mike, our zodiac driver, slowed down and approached the mystery object tentatively. "It looks like a tree trunk" said someone but this seemed unlikely to me as there are no trees in Antarctica. We drew nearer to the "thing", now reckoning that it was 40 to 50 feet long. As we were almost upon it, the object moved suddenly. Much splashing and spraying ensued. We had almost collided with a sleeping humpback whale! What a moment!

24. The Night was Silent: Botswana, Chobe Region

A surprising fact about African elephants is that, despite their massive size and weight, their footsteps are almost completely silent. Unless an elephant cracks a twig or rustles some leaves, you will not hear its footsteps. Apparently soft, spongy padding on the underside of an elephant's feet smothers any objects beneath it, causing nearly all noise to be muffled.

Deep in the forests of the Chobe region of northern Botswana, there are, even today, large numbers of elephants. Some 50 miles from any main road, I arrived at a private tented camp set in thick mopani woodlands. "My" tent stood on a raised wooden platform beneath a large, shade-giving tree overlooking a small lake. The tent was fronted by a generously sized veranda. The roof and sides were constructed from thick canvas and it had a proper wooden door. Mesh "windows" let light in and allowed the tent's resident to see out clearly. A large bull elephant was casually splashing around nearby in the shallow water, noisily ripping out clumps of reeds.

At the end of the first day in this lovely place, having enjoyed sun-downers and a congenial dinner, I retired to sleep around 9.30pm. The night was silent and peaceful. I drowsed off contentedly into a pleasant dream-like state.

About half an hour later, I was abruptly awakened from my woozy slumbers by the sharp cracking of branches and crunching of leaves. A bright moon lit up the otherwise dark sky. Through the mesh front "window" of the tent, I picked out the silhouette of an elephant's trunk waving up into the nearby trees.

All of a sudden, the elephant lumbered out of the gloom and presented himself directly outside my tent. He was huge! By now, I was wide awake and wide-eyed, sitting up on the edge of my bed, heart thumping. This was out of excitement, not fear, as I knew the elephant would have no interest in me (and in any case elephants are vegetarian!). As I watched, he stepped right up on to the tent's veranda. He could not have been more than ten feet away!

Listening intently, I could even hear him breathing. Quietly I surveyed his huge bulk as he swept the veranda with his trunk. Finding nothing to eat there, he stepped back down and strolled softly around the side of the tent where he proceeded to munch a small tree which stood just a few feet away. I could still see the outline of his huge mass through the mesh side of the tent.

Some minutes later and without warning, the elephant dissolved into the night and immediately the loud cracking and crunching noises ceased. Once again, the night was silent.

25. Roasted Rat Anyone?:
Laos, Luang Prabang

Laos is not your typical tourist destination – which is one of the reasons why I wanted to go there. And so I embarked on a river voyage on the upper stretches of the Mekong, heading north, ultimately up and over the border out of Laos and into southern China. This voyage of over 750 miles was in a small, traditionally-styled and very comfortable river-boat, built mostly out of teak wood.

The river was fascinating – at times it was narrow and rocky with fast rapids, whilst in other places, it would open out into a wide, smooth pond. Often the captain had to navigate in a zig-zag fashion to manoeuvre the boat past rocky outcrops and small islands. It was reassuring to learn that he had navigated this river for over 20 years. The steep slopes alongside were thickly forested, with occasional banana plantations, rubber tree forests and fields of rice or hops (destined mostly for the Chinese market). As the boat made its tortuous way northwards, high mountains provided a beautiful backdrop. On the river banks, local people used the fertile, silty soil to plant an array of vegetables in tiny, somewhat disorganised plots.

Upstream, we stopped for two days in Luang Prabang – this small city is a UNESCO world heritage site on account of its unique and well preserved architectural, religious and cultural heritage. What I loved most about it, however, was the multitude of intriguing colourful markets. The "night market", rather curiously, began during the day and all manner of weird and wonderful (and sometimes unmentionable) things were offered for sale there.

Wandering through the food market area with my friend Marion, I was bewildered, bewitched and bemused by the range of exotic and (for me) unrecognisable fruits and vegetables on display. Marion, who is an accomplished cook, was expertly and enthusiastically identifying the various colourful exhibits for me when – suddenly – she stopped, rooted to the spot, and shrieked: "O my God". The expression on her face was a mixture of shock, horror and disbelief. "What is it"? I asked fearfully. Was she having a heart attack, had she seen a ghost or was a marauding maniac about to attack us with a very large knife? "Look" she cried, pointing to a stall directly ahead of us.

And there it was. In the midst of a table-full of colourful vegetables rested a large rat!

It lay there upside-down with its legs in the air and mouth wide open next to some spring onions.

It was, of course, very dead.

As we cautiously approached, the lady stall-owner began to laugh heartily – no doubt at our horror-struck expressions. Recovering slightly, we both smiled back and a congenial, comfortable camaraderie was established. We subsequntly learned from the lady (who spoke good English) that Laotian people regularly eat rats and it is not considered to be unusual.

Roasted rat anyone? Perhaps not …

26. Frolicking Sea Lions: Sea of Cortez, Mexico

No specific activity had been planned for that afternoon. During the morning, our small expedition ship had progressed northwards as far as Isla Angel de la Guarda, the longest and second largest island in the Sea of Cortez (which separates the long, narrow Baja California peninsula from the Mexican mainland). Much of the shoreline was composed of dramatic cliffs and rock stacks of orange, peach, olive green and cream, each in distinct layers. A geologist's dream. The wind had died down and the sea was delightfully tranquil.

After lunch, the expedition staff asked the passengers if anyone wanted to venture out on a spur-of-the-moment zodiac cruise. We had had a strenuous morning climbing a hill over rocky, scrubby ground and ultimately scrambling up on to a steep ridge, and so most of my fellow passengers declined. Not me.

Six of us set out with Jenny who drove the zodiac (open, inflatable rubber boat). As we rounded the tip of a small island near where our ship was anchored, we saw that the long, rocky beach ahead of us was jam-packed with California sea lions, probably numbering into many hundreds.

California sea lions are highly intelligent and appealing creatures. These particular animals were contentedly relaxing on the rocky shoreline, perhaps enjoying an afternoon siesta, at least until they detected the droning of our boat's engine. All of a sudden, dozens of inquisitive heads popped up. Jenny slowed down, taking care not to venture too close. Fascinated, we watched the sea lions, wondering what might happen.

What did happen was astonishing and enchanting. Dozens of young sea lions dived in unison into the sea and began to zip and zoom alongside our zodiac. As Jenny increased our speed, they pursued us and began to porpoise, leaping out of the water in their enthusiasm to keep up.

After a few minutes of this frolicking behaviour, Jenny said "I wonder what they would do if we stopped". She brought the zodiac to a halt and switched off the engine allowing the boat to float gently.

Almost immediately, the sea lions stopped their porpoising antics, congregated around the back of the boat and popped their little heads up out of the water.

They gazed up at us with huge, appealing eyes.

Jenny turned the boat around and rocketed off again, back in the direction we had come. The young sea lions immediately proceeded once more to cavort excitedly alongside us, making lots of loud honking noises. I was quite certain that the expression on their little faces was one of pure glee.

As for me and my fellow passengers, we returned to our ship full of exhilaration, enthusiasm and exuberance.

27. Fire in the Sky: Costa Rica, Arenal

The volcano was shrouded in mist as we arrived at the Arenal Observatory Lodge, located high on a forested hillside directly opposite the mighty Arenal Volcano of Costa Rica. The lodge accommodation was delightful - private cabins were set in vast gardens in natural primary forest containing streams, waterfalls and well-maintained hiking trails. The Arenal Volcano appeared to be right on our doorstep even though there was a deep valley separating the Lodge from its fiery temperament.

From my cabin the view of the forest canopy and over the valley towards the volcano was glorious, even in misty conditions. The only sounds were the wind in the trees, the buzz of insects and the occasional chirping of birds. I loved this place already.

Having been dormant for hundreds of years, the volcano had unexpectedly and dramatically exploded into life in

1968 (although it has quietened down again in recent times). At the time I was there (in 2007), it was regularly spouting molten rocks.

I was tired that night and fell asleep quickly. Where possible, I like to sleep without curtains obscuring the view through my windows. Somewhere in the night, I was awakened – I didn't know why. Sleepily, I turned over and must have involuntarily opened my eyes. Through the panorama windows, I was astounded to see a red glow in the sky and what appeared to be fireworks tumbling out of the heavens. I wondered if I might be dreaming. The night was dark and slightly overcast, but the clouds were sufficiently high to reveal the silhouette of the great mountain opposite.

Entranced, I watched and listened. Pieces of fiery rock exploded into the sky, hurtled down the side of the mountain, crashed down to the ground and blasted back up into the air, only to smash down again. Loud popping and cracking noises resounded across the valley as further cascades of brightly lit molten fireworks tumbled down from the black sky. It went on and on, making the notion of going back to sleep somewhat superfluous. What a night!

28. Bandit: Guyana, Karanambu

Deep in the heart of Guyana at the top end of South America lies a place called Karanambu where savannah grassland, swamp and flood forest meet beside the Rupununi River. Karanambu Lodge was originally a working cattle ranch, but it is now an eco-lodge.

When I ventured into this remote area in 2009, I was extremely fortunate to meet Diane McTurk, a grand lady well-known for her work rehabilitating orphaned giant river otters. Diane's special relationship with the otters won her much acclaim, including tributes from Sir David Attenborough. Diane, who owned Karanambu Lodge, was my very gracious host for four delightful days.

My accommodation was in a spacious, clay-brick thatched cottage, with a veranda, twin beds and an attached washroom featuring a shower and flushing toilet. The windows were free of glass, allowing cooling breezes to enter through wooden slats. Early afternoon was siesta time.

A few months earlier, the camp staff had rescued an orphaned young raccoon, whom they had named Bandit. Bandit was largely allowed to roam freely around the camp and he tended to be inquisitive and mischievous. That afternoon, whilst I was resting, Bandit took it into his little head to visit my cabin. He cleverly squeezed himself in through the wooden slats at the front of the cabin and began to explore my table top. Hastily moving lotions, potions and hair brushes out of his way, I allowed him to investigate.

Bandit then took a particular liking to the bathroom and, to my huge amusement, not only inspected the shower area but also the toilet bowl and seat, turning himself upside-down into it, presumably to ascertain whether it might contain fish or some other type of edible delicacy.

Having established that no fish lived there, he clambered up on to the ceiling beams of the bedroom and postured and ponced about there for a while before frolicking noisily under the beds. He was generally a highly enjoyable and entertaining companion until he was eventually "rescued" by one of Diane's assistants.

One year later, I acquired a delightful little puppy, and decided to call him Bandit. He is as cute, characterful and mischievous as his namesake and is definitely not allowed into the bathroom!

29. Abandoned: Tanzania, Serengeti

The late afternoon sun was turning the parched earth into orange-gold. Our open safari vehicle was approaching a wide, dried-up river-bed. No rain had fallen here for several months, making life difficult for the wild animals of Tanzania. Our driver swung the vehicle gently to the right, carefully following a rough track near the upper rim of the river bed. Ahead of us, the river-bed was completely empty. Or was it?

What was that lying motionless on the ground? We approached slowly. "It's a baby zebra!" exclaimed one of my five fellow passengers. "It must be dead", said another. Slowly and silently we drew closer.

Without warning the "dead" zebra suddenly leapt to its feet, looked anxiously this way and that, disoriented and bewildered.

"He must have fallen asleep and been left behind by the herd", construed our guide. "O no, the lions will get him", said someone – we had seen a pride of seven lions a mile or two back.

We watched in silence, each of us feeling a mixture of sadness and apprehension for the forlorn, abandoned little creature.

A loud scuffling sound behind us caught my attention. "Look", I cried. There, on the far side of the river bed, two adult zebras had crashed down the embankment amidst a tornado of sand. Screeching to a halt, they eyed us suspiciously, stamping and snorting all the while. Then, deciding that we were probably worth ignoring, they galloped forward, bolted past our vehicle, reaching the baby a moment later.

There followed much snorting, sniffing and snuffling, as the two adult zebras checked the baby out. Then, accepting that he belonged to them, they turned around, and, together with their baby, took off at speed in the direction from which they had come, soon disappearing in a vast veil of sand.

For a moment, we all sat silent, contemplating what we had experienced. Inexplicably, I felt ridiculously happy.

30. Crossing the Arctic Circle: Norway

Many people don't realise that a large chunk of Norway lies above the Arctic Circle. The north-westerly coast of Norway is spectacularly mountainous and beautiful and it was here that I spent a week exploring the coastline and many offshore islands from a small expedition ship.

After a walk ashore through birch forest and around a pretty lake, we retraced our steps to board the ship's zodiacs (small, inflatable rubber boats) in order to return to the ship (or so I thought). I found myself unexpectedly in a zodiac driven by the ship's captain, Nils, along with one of the expedition staff and a pleasant English couple. Four other zodiacs completed the gathering.

Having boarded the zodiacs, we headed northwards on a silky calm sea, leaving the ship behind us.

Puzzled at first, I soon learned the purpose of this extended zodiac cruise.

Nils announced that we were approaching the Arctic Circle, that invisible line in the ocean which marks the border between the Arctic to the nor th and the Northern Temperate Zone to the south. Alternatively, it can be described as marking the northernmost point at which the top half of the midday sun is visible on the December solstice and the southernmost point at which the top half of the midnight sun is visible on the June solstice. Right now, we were close to the June solstice.

The fleet of five zodiacs extended in a straight, smooth line across the ocean, with our sturdy ship following behind. As if anticipating some great event, Nils produced a bottle and five glasses. He poured a generous quantity of neat Aquavit into each glass and handed them around.

Moments later, the great event was announced – we were about to cross the Arctic Circle! Glasses were quickly re-filled. Our five zodiacs floated gently together on a silken, silver sea surrounded by a raft of raucous black-backed gulls. The equally raucous passengers merrily scoffed Aquavit whilst at the same time wafting lyrically about the wonderfully beautiful scenery. It was super-fun!

31. Blue Whale Whirlwind: Mexico, Sea of Cortez

Travelling on a small expedition ship in the Sea of Cortez (which separates the Baja California peninsula from the western side of the Mexican mainland) is an absolute delight. This sea is one of the richest on the planet in terms of marine life. Many species of whale live here, some permanently and some seasonally. Humpback whales, orcas, fin whales, sperm whales, minke whales, pilot whales and the largest of all – blue whales - are all to be found, some in great numbers.

The blue whale is the largest creature to ever have lived on our planet. An adult blue can be up to 100 feet long - truly immense. Today the blue whale is an endangered species. Sighting one will inevitably be an exciting, awe-inspiring experience.

Ahead of our ship that day we saw not one, but two blue whales which appeared to be feeding. We approached slowly. "There's another one", cried one of my fellow-passengers. By now, all 80 or so passengers and 12 expedition staff were on the ship's outer decks, watching intently, cameras at the ready.

Astonishingly, there were six blue whales circling around – feeding on a massive shoal of krill, their main food. Even our experienced expedition leaders were astounded – none had ever seen so many blue whales all together. This was a rare and seriously thrilling encounter.

By now our small ship was directly alongside the six whales, who, obviously undaunted by our ship, were engrossed in their feeding frenzy. I fixed my eyes on one of the whales and watched her purposefully. My chosen whale had swum right up to the side of the ship directly below where I was standing. She then proceeded to swim outwards in a wide circle.

Diligently, she sustained her course of circling, now some way out from the ship, all the while blowing bubbles. She continued on around, turning back towards us.

Just before reaching the ship, there was an almighty splashing and thrashing as she opened her mighty jaws and gulped in a giant mouthful of food. There was a massive whirlwind of spray, froth and foam. Truly breathtaking!

The whale revelry continued for some time until, presumably, all the krill had been demolished. The blue whales then swept off into the wider ocean. As for us, we continued our voyage, enthralled and awestruck by what we had witnessed.

32. Wild Dog Chase: Botswana, Linyanti Area

Some people say they're ugly. But I think they are quite beautiful.

African wild dogs (also known as "painted dogs") live in family groups and are intelligent and highly sociable and caring of each other, always sharing their food and working together to care for their young.

It was the last day of my trip to Botswana – which is without doubt my favourite safari destination. Why? Because Botswana's government controls and limits the number of visitors - by restricting the number of lodges and camps that can be built in each of the wildlife areas. The safari outings are largely in open vehicles. As a result, the experience you get is far different and more intimate than can sometimes be the case elsewhere in Africa.

As usual, we rose early that day and ventured off in our open four-wheel drive vehicle. "We'll try to find the wild dogs", said Tomas, our guide/driver.

Having caught several tantalisingly close but fleeting glimpses of dogs running through the bush, we tried hard but without much success to follow them over the rough ground. We had almost given up and Tomas had bumped the vehicle out of the thick bush and back on to the "road". We sighed in disappointment.

Then it happened. Without warning, a full-sized male impala exploded out of the bush directly in front of us. Reacting instinctively, Tomas braked hard. Sensing the danger, the impala engaged his powerful hind legs to spring up – and up - and sailed, as if in slow motion, high over the bonnet of the vehicle, landing safely on the other side. Moments later, five wild dogs burst out from the bushes yipping and yapping excitingly and running at full pace in pursuit of the terrified impala. In a flash they were all gone. "Did that really happen?" asked the lady sitting next to me.

So did the wild dogs catch the impala? We learned a little later that they had not succeeded in that particular chase, but had found a meal elsewhere. The impala lived to see another day.

33. Starved in China: Dunhuang, China

Everything about our trip had been wonderful. Except one thing – the food. I had been travelling in western China for a week together with seven intrepid companions, plus an English guide and a Chinese guide. We had experienced some wonderful things – caves with prehistoric inscriptions, rock paintings, temples, mountain scenery, vast deserts and much more.

Back in 1996 when I made this journey, relatively few foreign visitors ventured this far west in China and so the infrastructure and facilities for travellers were either non-existent or extremely basic. Restaurants, such as they were, usually proffered only one meal, and it was always the same. There would be a large bowl of glutinous white rice, cemented into a single sticky block. Another bowl would be filled with a bland, wishy-washy mixture of suspicious looking vegetables swimming in a sort of gravy. No potatoes, no eggs (even at breakfast time), no bread and pretty much no meat. Occasionally, the "meal of the day" would be described as chicken stew, but it became obvious that whoever had prepared it had removed all the chicken from the scraggy creature's bones before preparing the dish for us. As a result, everyone in our group (except perhaps the Chinese guide who always ate separately from the rest of us) was suffering from under-nourishment and withdrawal symptoms.

And so it was that we arrived in the town of Dunhuang, an oasis city located farther to the east. It was early afternoon and after settling in to our comfortable hotel, we had agreed to meet up downstairs. But someone seemed to be missing. "Where's Dave", I asked. "Don't know", came the reply. Suddenly Dave burst into the hotel lobby, his face alight with enthusiasm, eagerness and exhilaration. "You'll never guess", he cried excitedly, "there's a western-style café-bar just down the road!" They are offering burgers, chips, pizza ...... Before Dave could utter another word, all seven of us jumped to our feet, and charged out of the hotel, hotly in pursuit of Dave, who valiantly led the way to the Manhattan Café.

The friendly local people eyed us up with great curiosity and amusement as we raced down the main street of

Dunhuang, ignoring vibrant market stalls, wonderful photographic opportunities, shops full of colourful trinkets and all possibilities to digest any local culture. A western-style café-bar! Wow!

We stampeded into the café, sat together at a large round table and grabbed menus. Menus? We hadn't seen one of these for over a week. Now, I have to say that normally - back home in bonny Scotland - I would tend to decline any opportunity to eat a burger. But needs must. Nine burgers, nine portions of chips (heaven!), several milkshakes, a pizza or two and large portions of ice-cream later, we all sighed with intense satisfaction. Aaahh!

Somewhat bizarrely, this unexpected episode turned out to be a highpoint of the entire tour!

34. Thunder at the Waterhole: Namibia, Etosha National Park

In northern Namibia, the vast Etosha National Park offers wildlife lovers an experience comparable to the very best Africa has to offer. Out on a morning safari drive in the eastern part of Etosha, Peter, our guide/driver, drove me and my two fellow travellers to the edge of a large waterhole. It was mid-December, and very hot. The seasonal rains had failed to materialise so far and so the land was dry, sandy and scrubby. In such conditions, a waterhole is an excellent choice for wildlife viewing as animals tend to congregate wherever there is water. On the other side of this waterhole, the bare land gave way to scrub which seemed to stretch all the way to the horizon.

The sun shone brightly from a cloudless sky. As we parked next to the waterhole, I was disappointed to see that there were no animals there. On the plus side, there were no other vehicles there either. The land was empty and silent.

"We'll wait here for ten or fifteen minutes" suggested Peter, "and if nothing comes, we'll move on". We waited. After about five fidgety minutes, I thought I detected a distant rumbling noise. "Thunder" I pondered, then immediately deduced that a thunderstorm was highly unlikely given the cloudless blue sky. But the thunder grew louder. "What is that?" I asked Peter. He just smiled knowingly.

Moments later, looking out towards the scrubby bushes beyond the waterhole, I detected clouds of sand swirling up from the parched ground. Was there a tornado approaching? Baffled, I continued to observe the sand storm and the thunderous rumbling which by now had substantially increased in volume.

And suddenly – there – beyond the waterhole – a mirage of elephants crashed out of the bush, running at full speed towards us from the far side of the waterhole.

Around seventeen thundering elephants, females and young, hurtled exuberantly into the water throwing up fountains of churned up mud with their huge trunks and bodies. They proceeded to splash, roll, spray and wallow in the water and mud, snorting and trumpeting jubilantly.

I knew that elephants loved water, but what I had not appreciated up until that day was how much sheer pleasure they can draw from it. What a joyous sight!

One large female elephant, however, most likely the matriarch of the herd, was apparently not entirely contented. She emerged from the water, faced our vehicle and flapped her huge ears, concerned perhaps for the safety of the young baby at her heels. She then advanced towards us - astonishingly close – perhaps about 10 feet away from the open vehicle. "Please sit very quietly", Peter advised us, "she's just checking us out". My heart beat rapidly for a few minutes as the elephant towered above us making low rumbling noises. But Peter was right. Deciding that we posed no threat to her or her baby, the huge matriarch lumbered off to re-join her family. The entire herd then proceeded to amble back into the bush, having drunk and bathed to their hearts' content. The thunderstorm was gone.

35. Under Attack: Mexico, Sea of Cortez

The Sea of Cortez in north-west Mexico is one of richest seas on the planet in terms of the numbers and diversity of marine life. Jacques Cousteau once referred to it as "the world's aquarium".

The guests on the 48-passenger ship on which I was travelling had been told that we were approaching a channel where dolphins were frequently sighted. I duly prepared my camera and positioned myself strategically on the front deck.

Some distance ahead, I could see that the sea was all churned up, bubbling like a boiling cauldron. Binoculars revealed a frenzy of pelicans and boobies diving into the ocean like darts, spearing the water with their fierce bills. Fish were being thrown up into the air amidst the chaos. Of course, where birds are feeding on fish, there might well be dolphins.

Indeed, as our ship grew closer, we could see that a very large pod of common dolphins was leaping, darting and racing about amidst the turmoil. Our expedition leader reckoned that there must be about a thousand of them taking part in the feeding frenzy.

Suddenly, as if someone had given a command, the dolphins stopped feeding, turned around and sped in unison straight towards our ship.

As they charged towards us, it felt like we were under attack! But the dolphins' mission was to have fun, not fight a battle.

On reaching the ship, they proceeded to bow ride, swim at high speeds alongside, dart in different directions, leap into the air and surf in the ship's wake. Wow!

They continued with their joyful game until the ship reached the end of the channel, then they sped off, heading back to their fish.

But that was not the end of the party. Our captain decided – for fun – to turn the ship around and cruise back down the channel the way we had come. Once again, the dolphins spun around and made a frantic dash towards the ship to fly alongside us, surf the ship's wake and bow ride. What joy!

36. Songs of the Rainforest: Peru

Nowadays, rainforests are in the news largely because of their creeping destruction and the disastrous consequences of that deforestation on our planet. Back in 1986, when I experienced a rainforest for the first time, that unfortunate phenomenon had not yet been contemplated.

I had flown eastwards - from Cuzco in Peru to a scruffy shanty town on the other side of the Andes mountains called Puerto Maldonado - which as far as I could tell was located in the middle of nowhere. From there, I journeyed upriver in a small speedboat for 35 miles to a remote lodge, overlooking the river and set deep in the rainforest. Needless to say, it was hot and humid. Unsurprisingly, it rains a lot in the rainforest.

I had the privilege to enjoy many experiences during my three-day stay in this remote place. But my most vivid memory is not what I saw there, but rather what I heard.

Settling down to rest during the hottest part of the day, but not feeling inclined to sleep, I lay quietly and listened. The sounds of the rainforest were mesmerising. Tropical birds cheeping, chirping, squawking, hooting and whistling, tree branches creaking and crackling, frogs croaking, monkeys howling, cicadas humming and buzzing and from the nearby lagoon, river otters chattering. It was hypnotic and simply enthralling.

37. Geysers, Mud and the Bear Man: Russia, Kamchatka Peninsula

Back in 1993, tourism in the far north-east of Russia was non-existent. The area was a major base for nuclear submarines and definitely not open to foreign visitors. The small expedition ship on which I would be travelling for the next few weeks was, I learned, the first ever foreign passenger ship to be permitted to visit Petropavlovsk, the main town of Kamchatka, a wild, remote and sparsely inhabited peninsula in the far north-east of Russia.

With a day in hand before the start of the voyage, I and a number of others were offered the opportunity to take an unscheduled helicopter excursion to the Valley of Geysers, hidden in a deep, remote part of Kamchatka's wild mountainous interior. This valley was discovered only in

1941 but little exploration of the area took place until 1972. Getting there necessitated a helicopter flight over tundra, forested hills, rivers and several active volcanoes. As we progressed farther and farther from the coast, patches of snow began to appear on the mountain tops. The helicopter flew low to allow its passengers close views of this vast untouched wilderness.

One and a quarter hours later, we landed in a meadow full of wild flowers and surrounded by high green hills. We walked across the meadow, then down over rough ground into the deep, steam-filled canyon.

Geysers were spurting their steaming water out of an assortment of craters and fissures on the sides and foot of the canyon.

I learned later that this valley has the second largest concentration of geysers in the world.

One geyser erupted directly in front of me, flinging its stream of white water high into the sky in a cloud of steam, before quietening down into a docile bubbling.

The sounds of the valley hissing and spluttering were mingled with the glurping and slurping of several strange, deep mud craters. This place was eerie, exciting and slightly scary. There were no fences back then, only a few paths and no restrictions as to where you could, or should, walk.

Unexpectedly we met a man there who had spent the previous 20 years in this area studying the enormous Kamchatka brown bears and their behaviour – a real-life mountain man of dark, rugged appearance and stocky build. He showed us a collection of spectacular photographs of "his" bears for which he was, I learned later, renowned throughout Russia. What a strange life he must have led during his summers there, alone in his basic one-room hut with only the bears for company.

I discovered later that our "bear-man" was Vitaly Nikolayenko, a self-educated researcher and photographer. Each year, he would spend many months in the wilderness, spending his days following the bears and documenting their feeding, mating and social habits. He also worked very hard to battle the illegal hunting of his beloved bears. His many hundred journals turned out to be one of the most important records of brown bear behaviour. Sadly, he was found dead ten years later in 2003, apparently as a result of a bear mauling.

Equally sadly, a massive mud-flow inundated two thirds of the Valley of Geysers in 2007. A spokesman for the World Wildlife Fund was quoted as saying: "This is tragic for humankind, in that we have lost one of the great natural wonders of the world". Nevertheless, the area was subsequently opened up again for tourism.

As for me, I was grateful to have had the opportunity to visit this spectacular wild place in its original natural, undeveloped state, as nowadays it has become yet another destination for organised tourism, and the wonderful "bear-man" is long gone.

38. Gannets Galore: St Kilda, Scotland

The islands of St Kilda lie far out into the Atlantic Ocean, about 40 miles west of Scotland's Outer Hebrides. Nothing lies beyond except North America. Wild westerly gales lash these isolated shores. Even in summer the weather can sometimes be ferocious.

Despite the remoteness and harshness of these far-flung islands, people lived on Hirta, St Kilda's main island, for over 4,000 years, exploiting the huge colonies of seabirds for food and oil. But by 1930, when only 36 people remained, life there had become unsustainable. The people voted to be evacuated, leaving these islands at the edge of the world empty and alone to brave the westerly gales. Now, St Kilda constitutes a dual UNESCO World Heritage Site and is managed by the National Trust for Scotland.

Today the only permanent inhabitants of St Kilda are seabirds which number nearly a million. Most live on the sea cliffs, which are the highest in the UK, or on high, rugged rock stacks. As well as 136,000 pairs of Atlantic puffins, one of the world's largest colonies of northern gannets, totalling 30,000 pairs, live and breed here. Gannets are the largest seabirds in the North Atlantic, having a wingspan of up to six and a half feet.

Travelling to this remote and rugged wild place on a small expedition ship, I had the good fortune to be able to land on Hirta to explore the beautifully restored village and walk up the steep hillside until without warning the ground gave way to sheer cliffs, forcing me to an abrupt stop.

On departing, our ship sailed towards and past the two dramatic, vertical rock stacks of Stac an Armin and Stac Lee. From the outside decks of the ship we could see dense throngs of gannets soaring in the sky above the stacks.

As we drew closer, an astonishing thing happened. Gannets in their hundreds flew out from the stacks straight towards our ship and began to circle around it – in a clockwise direction - all the time eyeing us up attentively.

Round and round they wheeled and glided – time after time after time. Some coasted past only just out of reach of the outstretched arm.

In my imagination, I fancied that the chief gannet must have declared "hey lads, there's a ship approaching, let's go check it out and have some fun". Because fun is what they were unquestionably having, as indeed we, the passengers, certainly were. This party lasted for over half an hour when the gannets, perhaps satisfied that they had seen us off successfully, headed back in a single massive flock to their rugged rock stacks.

We sailed away into the sunset, a ship full of very happy passengers.

39. Chance Encounter: Zimbabwe, Lake Kariba

The bush "airport" on the southern shores of Lake Kariba in Zimbabwe consisted of a dirt runway and a shack containing some rickety chairs where travellers could wait for the small bush plane to arrive – never knowing precisely when that might be.

I was seated opposite a middle-aged American couple who were not part of my small group of travelling companions. Of course people who involuntarily find themselves in close proximity to strangers tend to talk to each other. And so it was that I struck up a casual conversation with the American pair.

"Where are you from?" I enquired politely. "We're from Amarillo, Texas" said the woman. Carol, one of my fellow travellers who was sitting on my left, looked up with mild interest and interjected, "I have an aunt who lives in Amarillo, although I've never met her". There followed a moment's silence, during which I'm convinced we all had the same silly thought.

In that moment I briefly recalled a time some two years earlier when, on answering "Scotland" to the same question, another American woman replied "My daughter-in-law is from Scotland, you might know her ...." Apparently

77

she imagined that I must know every one of the five and half million people who inhabit Scotland ... Admittedly Amarillo has fewer than 200,000 people, but even so....

The moment's awkward silence passed and the American woman decided to take the risk. "What's your aunt's name?", she enquired cautiously. "Anne Charleston" revealed Carol, sounding unenthusiastic. The silence that followed wasn't won of awkward embarrassment, but rather of stunned astonishment. The American woman's mouth fell open and quivered precariously. Her husband stared at Carol, his eyes as wide as super-moons, seemingly in deep shock.

"But ... but ..." stammered the woman ... "but ... *I'm* Anne Charleston". Now it was Carol's turn to stare. After a few interminable moments, the American man turned to his wife and proclaimed triumphantly "I told you she looked like your sister". There followed tears of emotion and happy hugs as the fortuitous and highly unlikely reality of the situation sank in.

It happened exactly like that. Carol met her aunt for the first time in a shack in the middle of the African bush entirely by fortuitous accident. What are the chances of such an encounter? And, as I mused over that question, it occurred to me that if I hadn't ventured to strike up a spontaneous conversation with the American couple, they would never have known.

40. Land of Giants: Guyana, Iwokrama

Guyana is sometimes described as a land of giants. Giant river otters, giant water lilies, giant anteaters and giant waterfalls all exist here.   Tourism in this small South-American country is, however, not well-developed and facilities are sometimes fairly basic.

At Iwokrama Field Station, however, the eco-lodge accommodation was lovely – individual, comfortably furnished cabins were situated in expansive gardens overlooking the Essequibo River.   This cool, swirling river flowed quietly around the edge of the camp. An early morning boat trip provided the opportunity to admire the many flowering trees – reds, yellows and whites peppered amongst the greens of the rainforest.   Parrots squawked overhead, red howler monkeys howled through the trees (as their name would suggest!) whilst thousands of small insects skated gracefully across the water surface.

On arriving back at camp, I was astounded to see an enormous caiman stretched halfway up the pier gobbling up chunks of fish.

His huge, evil-looking jaws and razor-sharp teeth were rapidly demolishing the massive chunks.

Unsurprisingly, my fellow passengers and I were somewhat reluctant to exit the boat, given the proximity of this fierce-looking, prehistoric beast!

Our local guide, however, reassured us by explaining that this was "Eddie", the camp's "pet" caiman. Whilst still a youngster, Eddie had been accidentally struck by the camp's boat resulting in a serious injury to one of his back legs. This, the camp staff deduced, would have made his ability to hunt, and hence his survival, impossible. Feeling responsible for Eddie's misfortune, they had taken pity on him and resolved to support him by providing plentiful quantities of fish on the pier every day. Eddie had quickly learned where to go for his meals and tended to spend most of his time lurking in the dark waters near the pier in anticipation of his next meal.

Eddie was now a mature, fully-grown adult. Black caimans, which are found in many of the slow-moving rivers and lakes in the northern parts of South America, normally grow to around 13 feet in length. Eddie's body was most definitely longer than that. More noticeably, he was also very much wider in girth than a truly wild caiman would ever be. If he had been human, he would have been classed as obese. He was seriously enormous. A real Guyana giant!

41. Eighty Degrees North: Spitzbergen

Sailing again, we veered north-east, commencing our voyage along the far-northerly shores of Spitzbergen. We were at 80 degrees north, a mere 600 miles from the north pole. The evening was magically calm and peaceful.

After dinner, I decided that this was the moment to stay up on deck to experience the full effect of the midnight sun.

At that point, the sun was shining from a pale sky above a sea of rippled silk. I was at the top of the world amidst perfect and almost idyllic conditions – the contrast between my anticipated and assumed hostile weather and this actual peaceful idyll was astonishing. Amunsden once wrote: "In the light of the sun, the land looks like a fairy-tale. Pinnacle after pinnacle, peak after peak, crevassed, wild as any land on our globe, it lies, unseen and untrodden". Indeed this land looked like a fairy-tale to me.

The sun had veered around to the north, and as midnight approached, the small ship travelled on at minimum speed with hardly a whisper from the engines, nor a ripple in the water.

Sunlight glimmered and sparkled on a misty golden silken sea rippled with hues of orange.

A yacht drifted silently past.

The distant northern coast of the island of Spitzbergen floated above the mirage. It was sheer magic.

Midnight came and went under a golden yellow glow. Peace, perfect peace.

42. Eye of the Eagle: Isle of Skye, Scotland

Many years ago, my mother and I spent a winter weekend on the Isle of Skye. I was treating Mum to a short stay in a rather splendid hotel for her 80th birthday. On arrival there, I casually asked the receptionist if the hotel was busy, fully expecting the answer "no", given November is low season. "O yes", she said, "we have the hockey club in this weekend". "How jolly", I mused, and gave it no further thought.

The next morning over a sleepy breakfast, Mum suddenly declared "there's a big bird out there". Envisaging an oversized seagull or an unusually large pigeon (Mum was short-sighted), I mumbled something incomprehensible and continued devouring my porridge. "There's another one" she proclaimed defiantly. Still sceptical, I turned around. To my amazement, the hotel's front lawn was filled with beautiful birds of prey. Realisation dawned. It wasn't the hockey club staying here for the weekend, but the hawking club!

The weekend turned out to be highly entertaining - birds perching on the lawn, wings furiously flapping, aerobatics in the sky and even birds in the bar screeching intermittently whilst watching their owners downing pints of beer.

The highlight was Dillon, the golden eagle. With his owner's permission, I knelt down on the grass to photograph this magnificent creature eyeball-to-eyeball.

Dillon had completely mastered the art of the piercing stare. Arrogant, disdainful, superior.

Dillon glowered at me with his beautiful amber eyes, bringing me to the undeniable realisation that we human beings are truly a very inferior species.

43. Heart-stopping Moment: Kenya, Masai Mara

Lions are, in my opinion, lazy, languid and lethargic creatures. They spend most of their time asleep or else lounging around under a shady tree doing nothing in particular other than fending off flies. Except of course, when a male takes an interest in a female ...

In a lovely location in the Masai Mara where I was staying with my small group of intrepid fellow-travellers, we had already seen many lions, mostly slumbering under the shade of large trees. This time, however, it was different.

It began as a normal safari drive. Animals grazed as far as the eye could see. Zebra, topi, hartebeest, impala, gazelle, elephant and warthog were all sharing the same grass.

We had spotted a big male and a female lion some distance away resting quietly on the parched grass.

He was gazing lovingly at her.

As we watched, the female got up and began to strut off across the hillside. The male quickly followed her. Our driver/guide decided to change direction and drive around to the other side of the hillside, promising us that the lions were headed that way. He was right.

We stopped the open-sided vehicle in a convenient spot to watch them. Still a couple of hundred metres away, the female lion was plodding across the hillside with the male a little way behind, obviously intent on staying with her. They were headed in our direction. On and on they both marched. Suddenly, the female lion broke into a trot, then began to run at full speed. The male took a few moments to realise that his lady-love was absconding before he too launched himself into a sprint. By the time the female raced directly past our vehicle, there was some distance between the two.

The male lion was, by now, running at full speed, with his handsome mane flying in the wind and a determined, lustful expression on his face. From where I was seated at the side of the open vehicle, it appeared as if he was charging straight at me. Logic told me that it was the female lion he was chasing, but on the other hand my eyes were seeing a huge, aggressive, powerful lion launching itself directly and resolutely towards me at breakneck speed.

It was a heart-stopping moment!

44. Knobbly-Faced, Leathery-Skinned and Double-Chinned: Venezuela

We were entering Los Llanos (the plains) of Venezuela, a vast and remote region on the eastern side of the Andes mountains. The terrain had transformed from forested mountain to open savannah where only an occasional small village with grazing cattle and crops interrupted the vastness of these open plains.

Around lunchtime, we arrived at the entrance to Hato El Cedral Ranch, a working cattle ranch covering some 130,000 acres of the Venezuelan lowlands. As soon as we turned off the main road on to a dirt track leading to the ranch, we began to spot wildlife – to my astonishment, the plains were brimming with deer, iguanas, turtles, egrets, herons, magnificent scarlet ibis and many capybara (the world's largest rodent which looks a bit like an over-sized beaver but has the body-shape of a miniature hippopotamus). And we hadn't even arrived yet!

The ranch, which was to be my home for the next four days, provided basic but comfortable bungalow accommodation for about 30 guests, amidst a spacious garden area. As lunch was ready, the welcoming owners asked us to come to eat immediately after a quick freshen-up in our bungalows. Near my bungalow, a large owl sat sleepily in a palm tree, but I resisted the temptation to stop to photograph him, respecting the request to hasten to lunch.

Having stopped inside my bungalow only to deposit my bag, wash my hands and pay regard to a tiny frog in the bathroom, I hastened to re-open the door. I had already stepped outside before I saw it.

An enormous, brightly coloured male iguana with an extremely long striped tail, had plonked himself just a few feet away from my front door at the foot of the big tree that cast shade over my bungalow.

The iguana stood stock still, as if in a trance, and eyed me up shiftily.

What should I do? Should I try to step around him, perhaps risking being attacked, or should I forgo lunch? Was this knobbly-faced, leathery-skinned, double-chinned creature highly dangerous, or completely harmless? I laughed out loud at the silliness of this dilemma.

In the end, hunger won me over and I risked life and limb to creep past the iguana's glowering glances. Happily, he didn't move a muscle.

45. Shimmering Giants: Greenland, Disko Bay

I had travelled up the west coast of Greenland before. Towering, snow-covered mountain peaks, vast glaciers and deep fjords surely make this the most magnificent scenery in the world.

There are no roads here and so the only way to get around is by ship. And so it was that I travelled on a Russian research vessel (the *Akademik Ioffe*), heading for the wonderfully named Disko Bay on the west coast of Greenland and the town of Ilulissat set within the Bay. Ilulissat, also known as Jakobshavn, is located approximately 220 miles north of the Arctic Circle and has a population of around 4,500 people and almost as many husky dogs.

Just over the hill lies the Ilulissat Icefjord, a UNESCO World Heritage Site. Many miles upstream from the fjord's outflow sits the enormous Jakobshavn glacier (*Sermeq Kujalleq* in Greenlandic), reckoned to be the perpetrator of the fateful iceberg that sank the Titanic in 1912. This is the head of "Iceberg Alley", so called because the Jakobshavn glacier is the fastest-moving and most prolific iceberg-maker in the world. Every year, 35 billion tons of icebergs calve off the front of the glacier, float down the narrow channel and eventually pass out of the fjord near the town of Ilulissat. Some are so large that they cannot manage to navigate the fjord and get stuck on the bottom until following bergs crash into them and force them forward. The result is a bay full of giant icebergs waiting to be tipped out into the wider ocean.

Our captain informed us that we would arrive at Ilulissat and anchor in the Bay early the following morning. Full of excited anticipation, I slept restlessly – I had been here before and knew how beautiful it was.

Around 6.00am, bright sunlight squeezed through the cabin's curtains and roused me from my slumbers. Contemplating whether we might have arrived yet, I perceived that there was no ship's motion and no engine sound. Rising, I went to the window and threw back the curtains. Immediately, I was hit by the most dazzling display.

Shimmering white giants floated silently on a sea of deep blue silk. The sun was sprinkling sparkling diamonds on to the sea which was motionless under a cloudless, cornflower sky.

These massive glistening icebergs often tower up to a kilometre high, each encompassing sculpted turrets, steeples and spires. It was the most stunningly beautiful thing I had ever set eyes on.

Yes I had known what to expect at Ilulissat (at least so I thought), but the natural wonder of this vista excelled all my expectations by a very long stretch. I uttered "wow" out loud, awestruck and mesmerised.

It was a very long time before I could drag myself away from the cabin window to embark on the day's activities.

46. Jingle Bells: Myanmar, Irrawaddy River

Back in 1998 when I travelled upstream on the Irrawaddy river, tourism in Myanmar was not encouraged. But the people up-country were far removed from the politics of this beautiful country and without exception they were demonstrably welcoming and extremely happy to meet visitors.

My two-week voyage up the Irrawaddy was in a small boat, built originally in Scotland and brought to Burma in 1948 as a working cargo ship. Subsequently the boat had fallen into decay and had been languishing at the pier in Mandalay when it was "found" and bought by a Scottish businessman. He then refurbished and transformed it into a comfortable colonial-style passenger boat capable of accommodating about 30 passengers. The refurbishment was carried out almost entirely by local people.

It was coming up to Christmas.

Each day the boat would "dock" somewhere, usually near a village. The villagers would rush down to the river and quickly construct a set of rudimentary steps into the often steep, muddy river embankment, anxious to ensure our safe passage ashore. Everywhere we travelled, the people were exceptionally friendly and gentle – faces brimmed with smiles, children waved excitedly, grandmothers laughed at us and old men grinned toothlessly.

One of my fellow passengers, a jovial Welshman called Peter, liked to sing. One day, on being greeted ashore by a throng of cheerful children, he began to sing "Jingle Bells". The children loved it. Within a few minutes, they had mastered the words and were singing along excitedly and enthusiastically. They trailed after Peter everywhere as if he was the Pied Piper, begging him to sing it again, sing it again, sing it again ... Village after village, Peter the Pied Piper had a horde of happy children following him everywhere.

The many images of Myanmar remain fixed in my memory for all time – old temples, golden pagodas, colourful markets, horse-drawn carts, trishaws, canoes, river barges and rafts carrying a multitude of strange cargoes, wonderfully soft colour effects on the river at sundown, sandbanks, bamboo houses, villages full of wide-eyed, laughing children.

But none of the images is as vivid as the throngs of children following behind Peter singing "Jingle Bells".

47. The Smoke that Thunders: Zimbabwe

At Victoria Falls, the mighty, mile-wide Zambezi river plunges and shatters 350 feet into a deep, narrow gorge, sending millions of rain-drops high into the sky. This incredible spectacle is at its most dramatic towards the end of the wet season when the river is at its raging highest.

The Falls, which lie on the border between Zimbabwe and Zambia, are known in the local language as "The Smoke that Thunders". That name is very apt.

On the opposite side of the narrow gorge into which the Falls plunge, the land sits at about half the height of the Falls, allowing the viewer to look both up and down at the raging torrent.

If you walk in the forest there, you are inevitably going to get wet.

But this is a phenomenon not to be missed.

The power created by the waterfall crashing into the narrow chasm far below creates "rain" which is thrown skyward by the sheer intensity and power of this mightiest of African rivers.

The afternoon I spent there was like strolling in Fairyland. Thousands of instant rainbows magically appeared and danced mystically around the bases of the trees, only to disappear again as soon as I drew near. The sun shimmered hot through the tree-tops whilst cool "rain" thrown up by the Falls misted down on to my head and shoulders like cascading drops of silk. What I was seeing and feeling was bewildering – the cloudless blue sky was sprinkling me with soft rain. Logic told me that was impossible, yet that is what I was experiencing. The combination of hot sun and cool rain striking my skin simultaneously was extremely sensuous and quite magical.

48. A Million Stars: Damaraland, Namibia

Namibia is a wonderfully diverse country with vast open spaces, astonishing rock formations, ancient rock engravings, abundant wildlife, moonscape-like canyons, a wild Atlantic coastline and the highest sand dunes in the world.

Westward and northward from the vast, wildlife-rich Etosha National Park lies Damaraland, a sparsely populated, mountainous semi-desert region. Scattered farms, each consisting of a muddle of mud and corrugated iron huts, a few windmills and the odd flock of goats occasionally interrupted my journey through this stunning landscape.

I was travelling with two other people and a driver/guide. Leaving our small road vehicle, we transferred to a four-wheel drive truck which took us 12 miles or so to our bush-lodge destination amidst peculiarly-shaped hills. This journey took over an hour as the terrain was steep and rough.

"Our "bush lodge" consisted of basic safari tents and separate open-air bucket showers.

This was not just like being in the middle of nowhere, it *was* the middle of nowhere! We were far, far away from any human "civilisation".

It was Christmas Eve. We four were alone in the camp with John, the camp manager and a small number of camp helpers. After dinner, we enjoyed animated conversation about the merits and demerits of travelling to wild places. "It's the bugs that put me off" said Helen, one of my fellow travellers. "There are no bugs here just now", declared John, "because it's so dry". We glanced suspiciously at each other, seriously doubting this unexpected proclamation. "See", said John and pointed to the light above us (powered by a generator). "If there were any insects here, they would be flocking to that light". Indeed, there were no insects to be seen. John then invited us to walk outside. Puzzled, we followed him. "Now listen", said John, as if proud of his undoubtedly superior knowledge. "Can you hear anything?" There was absolutely no sound, no buzzing, humming, chirping, croaking or whirring. Complete silence. There were indeed no insects whatsoever in this strange, silent land.

Several celebratory glasses of wine later, we all retired to our respective tents. Around three in the morning, I woke up realising that my over-indulgence in fine wine had triggered a need to visit the bathroom, which was located 30 or so metres away. Rising grumpily, I unzipped the front of my tent trying to remember which path to take. Stumbling outside, I was so astounded by the scene in front of me that I had to sit down on the ground, almost collapsing in the process. But why?

Above me, a million stars sparkled and shimmered down from an infinitely vast black sky. They appeared so close that I felt I could reach up and touch them. I recalled what John had said about how dry and unpolluted the Damaraland mountain air was and how far away we were from any town, village or other source of artificial light.

The camp's generator had been switched off when we retired to our tents and so there was nothing to interfere with the brilliance of the night sky. I must have sat, motionless, outside my tent for half an hour before I could bring myself to move. Nothing I had ever seen could compare to this. A million stars and a million "wows"!

49. Dawning of a Decade: Nepal

Ensconced in a small hotel in Kathmandu along with seven travelling companions on New Year's Eve, I asked Jim, our guide: "How are we going to celebrate New Year"? The Nepalese people don't celebrate New Year and so nothing was happening at the hotel.

Then I had an idea .....

At 04.30am, we boarded a small bus and drove up the mountain-side to reach a place called Nagakhot. We arrived at first light with the outline peaks of the Himalayas rising dusky and dramatic before they turned pink just before sunrise. By the time we had climbed to the top of a small hill, it was approaching six-o'clock. It was at that time that the midnight bells would be ringing back home. A six-hour time difference meant that we could celebrate the new year - and the dawning of a new decade - as the sun was rising over the Himalayas! It was a startlingly clear and crisp morning with stunning views across to folds and folds of high mountain peaks, including the magnificent Mount Everest itself.

Jim had brought ample supplies of food and drink along with us anticipating that these would be much appreciated in the cold early-morning mountain air. Which they certainly were. There were flasks of hot chocolate, delicious cakes and, importantly, an ample supply of local rum. These we spread out on our chosen hill-top.

At 6.00am exactly, we joined hands in a small circle and sang Auld Lang Syne – at least after a fashion. This caused much amusement among some local children and a group of baffled Japanese people who proceeded to compete with us by executing a tuneless version of "happy birthday". As the sun rose above the high mountain peaks beyond, we scoffed the rum with the hot chocolate acting to warm us up. Finally we relaxed for a bit, with the sun up now, dispersing a pleasant warmth across the erstwhile chilly morning.

The valley beneath us was perfectly tranquil, enhanced by some haunting local music emanating from a cluster of houses below. It was a very special and moving experience.

50. A Whale of a Tale: Baja California, Mexico

I had read the brochure and seen the photographs - happy people in small, open boats with whales alongside, within touching distance. "You would have to be exceptionally lucky to have that experience" I had thought, but I booked the trip anyway.

Sailing north from Magdalena Bay on the wild Pacific coast of the Baja California peninsula in north-west Mexico, we were headed for San Ignacio Lagoon, one of three sheltered, shallow lagoons where grey whales give birth to their calves in January each year. These lagoons are the only places in the world where grey whales give birth to their babies. The whales remain in these lagoons until the calves are strong enough to undertake the long migration north to their feeding grounds in the Bering Sea, a hazardous journey of over 10,000 miles.

Sometime during the night, we arrived and anchored outside the lagoon. Four open zodiacs (small inflatable boats) set out to enter the lagoon at 7.00am. Very soon, a whale was sighted, then another, and another. Whales and their calves were everywhere, rising slowly to the surface, rolling over, tail-fluking and "spy-hopping" (coming up out of the water head first). Soon my zodiac was in the midst of a group of these gentle, 40-foot giants.

Suddenly, a whale and her calf advanced towards my zodiac. I saw her tail surface some 25 feet away and at the same time felt her head bumping up against the underside of the boat.

To my amazement, she began to rub herself against the side and underside of the zodiac, now and again rising up

head first beside us to take a look before gently sinking back down, only to re-emerge at the other side of the boat.

But that was just the start. As soon as one mother and calf swam away, another pair would come round and begin to interact with us. I watched, mesmerised, as the adult whales gently pushed their calves towards us, coercing them into touching the zodiac. It was a game which they were obviously relishing! And because both the mothers and the calves lifted their heads out of the water right next to the zodiac, it was possible to reach out and touch them. The young whales had smooth, cool, skin that felt like the outside of a wellington boot, whilst the heads of the adult females were largely covered in harmless barnacles. Time after time, I was able to reach out and touch a real, wild whale. Wow!

Rolling and twisting about in the water, whales continued to surge around us, frequently swimming underneath the boat and gently caressing their huge bodies against it. On one occasion, an over-exuberant whale underneath us caused the zodiac to rotate around unexpectedly! Often, a whale would surface next to the boat and exhale vigorously, causing showers of salt-sea water and much hilarity.

These gigantic, gentle and totally wild creatures had chosen to interact with us and to return repeatedly to be petted and stroked. The party went on and on until eventually we had to return to the ship to begin the long voyage back south.

But I took with me some unforgettable memories of a most extraordinary encounter. Wow!

About the Author

Lynda Gordon is a semi-retired employment law specialist who, during her working career, had 20 business books published on various aspects of employment law. With more time to spend on personal interests, she decided to venture into a different style of writing.

Apart from travel to remote, far-flung places and a love of wildlife, Lynda's interests include photography, gardening, genealogy research, creative crochet and playing the concertina. She lives in a quiet coastal town in Aberdeenshire in Scotland along with her husband, Keith, and two small dogs.

Lightning Source UK Ltd.
Milton Keynes UK
UKHW021116030720
365931UK00009B/438

9 781839 750083